AF567133

The vast majority of the public who come into a museum don't know, but want to know. Most are seeking knowledge in the most general sense. People don't carry around art-history books in their back pockets. (N. Serota, Tate Gallery, London)

THE LANGUAGE OF ART FROM A TO Z

(writ in plain English)

N.E. Lahti

THE LANGUAGE OF ART FROM A TO Z

(writ in plain English)

York Books
12755 SW Wheat Grass Loop
Terrebonne, Oregon 97760

Revised Edition

ISBN 0-9620147-3-7

Printed in the United States of America

Table Of Contents

Preface

The principal reason for writing *The Language of Art from A to Z* is to set out and clarify terms commonly used in the art world, with plain English as its vehicle.

This book is intended to provide easy alphabetical reference for the student of art appreciation, **of whatever age**, and to communicate to those persons who would like to know more about art that language need not be a barrier to understanding it.

As an introduction to the language of art, the most well-known and influential art movements of the Western world are described as succinctly as possible. Brief essays on art from various parts of the world or from centuries past are presented with a bird's-eye view of history.

Artists named in the respective schools or movements are only representative and are not meant to be inclusive. References placed at the end of definitions are meant to guide the reader to other art terms, movements, or cultural ages.

The writer wishes to point out that critics and historians may have different points of view when interpreting the language of art.

A

Aboriginal Art

The Aborigines of Australia are creators of the world's longest continuous art tradition. Rock engravings and paintings from 60,000 years ago can still be seen on sandstone escarpments.

Art was used mostly as a means of communicating stories and for sacred iconography. Many art forms related to ceremonial rites: body painting, carved figures, decorated stones, and rock and bark paintings, as well as the "X-ray" style of simultaneously depicting both the insides and outsides of humans and animals.

Art in the 20th century has been cited as the single major industry for the Aborigines. During the recent past, artists have adopted new techniques and media, transferring their skills from ceremonial rock, bark, body, and ground paintings to canvas, board, prints, wood sculptures, and dyed textiles, with styles and subject matter varying across regions and tribal groups.

Artists, especially in urban areas, have used a variety of media to create political and cultural statements about their ancient heritage and about themes such as land rights and racism. See Cave Art and Oceanic Art.

Abstract Art

Several of its principal motifs:

- The reduction of everything to concrete, essential form.
- The theory that color and form have their own qualities.
- The absence of realistic detail.
- Imagery that is simplified, distorted, or exaggerated.
- Penetration into the world of mystery to discover the basic truths of life.
- Exploration of the fourth dimension through a higher consciousness.
- A field of action.
- A zone of silence.

Two important divisions:

A. Abstract Expressionism — A painterly, soft-edge style. Spontaneity is its primary source of expression. Brushwork often appears dynamic and aggressive. (Its major approaches: action painting, large color fields, and abstract or expressive figuration.) See Abstract Expressionism.

B. Geometric Abstraction — A linear, hard-edge style. It is marked by clarity and precision. Color is often used to emphasize structure. See Geometric Abstraction.

Kandinsky (1866-1944), the author of *Concerning the Spiritual in Art* (1912), is recognized as the first to establish Abstract art as a unified and authentic style of expression. It was his wish to elevate the human spirit by dematerializing representational objects into symbols in the belief that pure form and pure color would make "sounds" that would reverberate into the soul. See *Improvisations*.

As a note to history, Abstract art is the 20th century's most distinctive movement because prior to 1900 there was no thought of painting a picture that did not represent something such as a face, a body, or a landscape.

Abstract Collage

Schwitters (1887-1948), known as a pioneer of this art form, described his work as "a kind of visual poetry." He constructed his art from bits and pieces found in the streets: anything that had been thrown away he collected and transformed into collages combined with paintings of nonfigurative forms. Schwitters called his productions *Merzbau* and *Merzbilden* and queried: "What is art? What isn't?" He was a tireless advocate of Dada.

Abstract Expressionism or The New York School (1940s-1950s)

A title that does not refer to any one particular style; rather, it places emphasis on personal expression, especially as seen in Action Painting.

This school changed the direction of Western painting: the art of painting seemed to be reinvented. It developed into the most powerful, original movement in the history of American art and, for the first time, American art became a dominant force.

Between 1942 and 1946, the modern art gallery and museum, Art of This Century, owned by Peggy Guggenheim, exhibited the artworks of Baziotes, Hofmann, Pollock, and others. It was during this time that Abstract Expressionism was launched. DeKooning and Pollock were its most powerful influences.

The following artists are regarded as the first generation of the New York School.

Hofmann (1880-1966)
Tomlin (1899-1953)
Rothko (1903-1970)
Gottlieb (1903-1974)
Gorky (1904-1948)
Still (1904-1980)
DeKooning (1904-1997)
Newman (1905-1970)
Krasner (1908-1984)
Kline (1910-1962)
Pollock (1912-1956)
Baziotes (1912-1963)
Guston (1913-1980)
Motherwell (1915-1991)

Over the years, the term "Abstract Expressionism" has overshadowed a wide range of styles, both established and emerging. See Abstract Art, Action Painting, Art Informel, Color Field Painting, Drip Painting, Figurative Expressionism, and Stain Painting.

Abstract Formalism

Artists based their work on symbolic form in the belief that such compositions would help viewers perceive truths the artists had captured. They believed their representations of pure form was the only true art: complete nonobjectivity was their motif. See Formalism, De Stijl, and Suprematism.

Abstraction-Création (art nonfiguratif) (1931-1936)

A nonfigurative painting and sculptural movement founded to reflect the ideals of Abstract art. Its primary intention was to encourage Geometric Abstraction in all forms. At one time it had over 400 adherents.

Academic Machine

A technical exercise demonstrating the painter's degree of skill in manipulating the standard techniques of drawing, painting, and arranging a picture according to established formulas. (The sterility of much academic art lay in the fact that it copied other art, rather than creating a fresh vision.) See Pompier Painting and Salon Painting.

Academy Art or Academic Tradition

Marked by traditional draftsmanship, somber color, and beauty along with classical ideas or historical themes. The artist Reynolds (1723-1792), as the first president of the Royal Academy of Art in England, expounded academic doctrine: the rules of good taste, acceptable technique, and the importance of authority in art, with selected subject matter as only proper for great art. After the French Revolution of 1789, artists began to experiment and to launch new movements. Disregard for traditional subject matter evolved: artists felt free to choose as their subjects anything that appealed to the imagination and aroused interest. See Grand Manner and History Painting.

Academy Figure

As a technical exercise, students render careful drawings or paintings of a nude figure; the figure, shown in heroic posture, is generally less than half life-size. This practice dates back to the 1500s.

Academy of Art

A term taken from antiquity. It was thereafter used by informal groups of artists in the 1400s in Italy who met for discussions. Official academies were established in Rome and Florence in the 1500s. The Royal Academy of Painting and Sculpture, founded in Paris in 1648, established a strict regimen that set the pattern for future academies. See Salon Painting.

Acrylic

A clear plastic used as a medium or vehicle for pigments that can be used on almost any painting surface in any thickness and in a variety of finishes. It combines the plasticity of oils with the precision and quick-drying capabilities of tempera and gouache.

Plexiglas and Lucite are the new materials of sculpture.

Action Painting or Gesture Painting (synonymous with Abstract Expressionism)

A term coined by the critic H. Rosenberg in 1952 to describe art based on movement: paint is applied in rapid, forceful strokes in order to show art as "pure life." In essence, a continual search for expression: some inner necessity or struggle is the artist's creative force. See Drip Painting.

Aerial Sculpture

A concept in which the space in and around a sculpture is as important as the artwork itself. Sugarman (1912-   ) was one of the first Americans to regard the entire surrounding space as integral to sculpture. See Constructivism.

Aesthetic Movement

During the period of the American Renaissance, this movement emphasized the importance of art decoration. At its most refined, the aesthetic taste sought decorative schemes in which wall treatments, textiles, and art furniture — in conjunction with a variety of objects such as art glass and art pottery — created a sequence of patterned surfaces.

Aesthetics

A term attributable to Aristotle. The Greek term means "of or pertaining to things perceptible to the senses," as distinguished from those learned by the intellect. Otherwise:

- Referring to a philosophy applied to art in an attempt to understand its qualities.
- The study of the creation, appreciation, and critical thinking of art.
- A sensitivity to beauty.

Whistler became a leading figure of an aesthetic movement whose credo was that artistic sensibility is the only thing in life worth taking seriously.

AfriCobra (African Community of Bad Relevant Artists) (1960s)

A militant group of black artists founded in Chicago to establish a contemporary black aesthetic derived from traditional African art and black American culture. Self-identity was its objective. Its principles: Free Symmetry, Shine, Awesome Imagery, and Koolaid Colors.

"Art for the People" became the motto for recent generations of black American artists.

After

Referring to the style, copy, or reproduction of an artwork. Occasionally, when an artist's work became well known or well liked, other artists would continue his style. See Caravaggisti and Giotteschi.

Leonard (1933-   ), an English portraitist, depicts his subjects after the style of master artists from centuries past, according to his interpretation of the subject's facial characteristics and according to certain timeless elements.

Airbrush

A relatively new tool, similar to a spray gun, used most often by commercial artists. Its primary purpose is to produce smooth gradations of color and tone.

Alla Prima/Au Premier Coup (at first)

A painting completed at one sitting, giving the impression of strength and spontaneity.

Allegorical Painting

Narrative art in symbolic form, a technique of ambiguity used in literature as well. Basically, it refers to a secondary meaning conveyed by symbols and allusions somewhat difficult to understand. One of the most famous is *The Sacred Allegory* by Giovanni Bellini (1430-1516). Its meaning is still being debated. See American Allegory.

All-Over Painting

A term associated with large Abstract Expressionist paintings in which color and rhythm are the forces of the artist's expression.

Allusive Painting

A term that relates to Abstract art: although the portrayal of the subject is changed, there remains the allusion to reality. See Illusionistic Painting.

Alogism

Malevich (1878-1935) is known for his alogical paintings in which diverse and incongruous images are juxtaposed in a manner resembling collage.

Altarpiece (Retable) (A religious work placed above and behind the altar)

During the Middle Ages, retabli (multi-panel altarpieces), which often measure ten to 15 feet high, were created as objects of devotion and to catechize believers through pictorial stories that concern key events in the lives of Christ and Mary, including the portrayal of biblical figures.

Retabli were usually collaborative workshop productions: the tasks of building, carving, priming, and gilding the panels, as well as some of the painting, were performed by members of the workshop who specialized in these areas. Different masters and workshops had their own techniques. See Isenheim Altarpiece.

Alternative Spaces or Artists' Spaces

In an effort to bypass the commercial gallery system, artists (mostly women) have formed co-op galleries. The primary purpose of the co-op movement is to provide a more democratic way to show work and to circulate ideas. Studios, the outdoors, and public areas are other spaces. See Kunsthalle.

American Abstract Artists (1936-early 1940s)

An association formed in New York City that promoted and annually exhibited Abstract art of every kind, with particular emphasis on Geometric Abstraction. They once picketed the Museum of Modern Art in Manhattan to demand that it exhibit American art. It became active again in the 1950s.

American Allegory (late 1700s-1800s)

An important function of allegory is to embody abstract ideas in concrete form. Classic of American allegory are prints that appeared everywhere, in a variety of forms, reflecting national principles, historic events, and celebrated heroes. These instructional and moralistic pictures helped create a shared mythology that both united a people and shaped a nation.

American-Art Union

Beginning in 1839, this union distributed thousands of etchings, paintings, and sculptures to subscribers by lottery. It played a vital role in American art because it did much to bring genuine artworks, by known or unknown artists, to the general population. Through the union's efforts, the idea that art was for everyone was planted in the public mind.

The union was dissolved in 1852 when the operation was declared illegal, but its success led to the establishment of smaller art unions.

American Fakirs, Society of (1891-1915)

A group of students at the Art Students League of New York, who held auctions, balls, exhibitions, and parades to raise money for scholarships. The students themselves produced parodies of important artworks, making fun of the work of contemporary artists. Materials used, such as ephemera, fabric, and food, to create three-dimensional pictures, were unusual for the times.

American Gothic

This classic American painting by Wood (1892-1942), depicting a Midwestern farmer and his spinster daughter, has been parodied many times by other artists.

American Impressionism

Although few Americans fully embraced the French style of broken color and dissolution of form, they did paint their themes from the everyday world, adapting an informal and intimate manner and rejoicing in the pleasure of color.

Cassatt (1845-1926), an expatriate, was the first American associated with Impressionism. She was largely responsible for introducing paintings of the French artists to the US. While the American artist Hassam (1859-1935) was in Paris, he adapted the techniques of Impressionism to street scenes. Upon his return to the US, he pioneered in advocating this style.

The art dealer Durand-Ruel was also responsible, in large part, for the widespread publicity that Impressionists received when he brought about 300 paintings from Paris to New York in 1886. See Art Dealer.

About 1890, members of the then-unformed group The Ten began to use the techniques of Impressionism. Many regional schools arose, including the Boston School and the Old Lyme Painters in Connecticut. See California Impressionism, Giverny Group, Hoosier School, and New Hope School.

American Indian Art

See North American Indian and Eskimo Art.

American Landscape Paintings

The creation of paintings to celebrate the landscape of North America. Luminism was a special quality used to enhance color of the natural world. Another quality was grandeur which seemed to reflect the growing nationalistic spirit of Americans, who were in awe of the wilderness and its beauty.

Doughty (1793-1856) is generally recognized as the first American to specialize in plein-air painting. See Hudson River School, Luminism, Marine Painting, Taos/Santa Fe School, Western and Indian Painting, and White Mountain Painters.

American Primitives

See Limners.

American Realism (1900-1915)

Many artists, including members of The Eight, apprenticed as newspaper and magazine illustrators. They concentrated on the city, portraying its vitality and its seamier side. Current events, social/political ideas, the labor movement, immigration, the writings of literary contemporaries, etc., were subjects of interest to them: they were committed to creating art about life.

Henri (1865-1929) and his colleagues pronounced: "Art that expresses the spirit of the people of today is the only necessary art." See Realism.

American Renaissance (1876-1917)

This term came into usage in 1880, and defines the work and interests of painters, sculptors, architects, and craftspersons, as well as politicians, financiers, industrialists, and others.

Architecture dominated the American Renaissance: monumental buildings decorated with murals and sculptures became part of the American landscape. Classic are The Library of Congress and the Boston Public Library.

According to popular ideas, art of the past would provide a useful source for the development of an intensely nationalistic American art: messages of patriotism and citizenship were implicit in public art and architecture. Paintings and sculptures of the human figure, whether nude or draped, were representative of some abstract allegory or a real person symbolizing high virtues.

When the Colonial period and the Revolutionary and Civil Wars entered the realm of history, paintings, plazas, monuments, memorials, tombs, and statues were created as symbols for American civilization, based on the classical past of Europe.

Over a period of two decades, numerous expositions brought the American Renaissance to people of all classes, which resulted in the creation of many art organizations and the founding of museums and art schools.

With the founding of new schools, societies, and clubs, new principles of study were established: artists sought inspiration from the history of art, notably the Italian Renaissance. Arcadian themes, myth, literature, and poetry inspired the artists. (Some critics, however, claimed art of this period had little to do with the actual life of the nation's citizens.)

During this era, an aesthetic movement was born; it was more an impulse than a style, and manifested a desire to get away from the ornamentation of the Victorian era. Artists, craftspersons, and architects were concerned with mural painting, sculpture, stained glass, furniture, textiles, tiles, and various collectibles: a conscious unity of all art forms evolved.

It was not until after WWI that art and culture ceased to be based on the past. A new generation of artists viewed images of the American Renaissance in an unfavorable light.

American Scene Painting (1920s-1930s)

The term "American Scene Movement" was adopted in 1933 by the government as its theme for the economic recovery of the US. Two major areas were covered:

1. Regionalism, in which concern for the native environment was embodied in portrayals of American life in certain regions.
2. Social Realism, in which the American scene was no longer idealized: the visual arts paralleled the realistic, humanitarian themes of authors such as William Faulkner and Sinclair Lewis.

American Scene artists tried to establish a truly American style: urban realists depicted scenes from America's cities, incorporating new technology and the effects of modernization on society; regionalists from the Midwest often portrayed rural life, capturing the great breadth and richness of America's countryside. See American Realism, Ash Can School, The Eight, 14th Street School, Regionalism, and Social Realism.

American School

Copley (1738-1815)
West (1738-1820)
Peale (1741-1827)
Stuart (1755-1828)
Trumbull (1756-1843)
Allston (1779-1843)
Audubon (1785-1851)
Morse (1791-1872)
Mount (1807-1868)
Bingham (1811-1879)
Homer (1836-1910)
Eakins (1844-1916)
Marin (1870-1953)
Sloan (1871-1951)
Bellows (1882-1925)
Benton (1889-1975)
Wood (1892-1942)
Marsh (1898-1954)

American Tonalism (1880-1915)

A school of American landscape painting. Like the Impressionists, the Tonalists were primarily interested in expressing the mood of light and atmosphere in nature. They preferred, however, to paint the quiet times of days and seasons when the world presented only a limited scale of colors.

Anatomy

Medieval artists discovered that by studying the anatomy of the human body they could achieve greater realism. With the arrival of the Renaissance and its emphasis on human achievement and perfection, interest in anatomy increased. Master painters, notably Leonardo da Vinci and Michelangelo, attended medical schools and autopsies. Ultimately, the subject of anatomy became integrated into the art-academy curriculum.

Ancients, The

A group of English artists who gathered around Blake (1757-1827). They painted with an imaginative vision using biblical stories, allegory, and poetical themes as their subjects. Blake believed himself to be under heavenly guidance and that it was the artist's duty to make his visions real to others.

Animation Art

Basically, it is painting on a transparent piece of plastic, originally hand-painted or hand-inked on celluloid. In more recent years, although acetate is the material commonly used, it is generally referred to as "cel." Various types of cels include Courvoisier, Limited Edition, Production, Sericel, and Publicity Cel.

The least expensive are Sericels (images that are silk-screened on acetate) which are reproduced in editions by the thousands. Limited Editions and Production Cels are rarer and of better quality and have sold for prices anywhere from several hundred dollars to thousands of dollars. Those most highly valued are original cels (individual celluloid frames).

Mickey Mouse, Woody Woodpecker, Tom & Jerry, and Bugs Bunny are among the many favorite characters depicted in Animation art.

During the making of *Snow White and the Seven Dwarfs*, the film producer Walt Disney employed 750 artists, perhaps making it the largest collaborative art project in the US. See Storyboard Art.

Antiquity

Referring to the period of about 500 B.C. in Greece up to the years before the Middle Ages.

Antropofaunas

Millares (1926-1972) created a series of paintings using red painted rags, rough textiles, scribbled forms, and the like.

Apocalypse, The

This masterpiece of 14 full-page woodcuts by Dürer of the German School, who was known as "the Leonardo of the North," illustrates the Revelations of St. John concerning the end of the world. It is universally believed the graphic virtuosity of this master artist has never been surpassed. Dürer also stands alone in Northern European art for the range of his subject matter. See Woodcut.

Applied Art

Art that is applied to the design and decoration of useful objects and to lettering and illustration in an attempt to unite the aesthetics of the fine arts therewith. Commercial art is regarded as a branch of Applied art. See Graphic Design and Industrial Design.

Appropriated, Appropriation

The reworking of art of the past by contemporary artists: an artist adopts another artist's imagery or style.

Aquarelle

The use of transparent watercolors. Also, an artwork so produced.

Arabesque

A curvilinear, rhythmic, decorative pattern of interwoven lines. Outlines of flowers, fruit, and animals are often used.

Arcadian Art

A scene depicting simple pleasure and quiet. The contemplation of pleasure in nature was broadened by 19th-century idealized art.

Archipentura

A title given by Archipenko (1887-1964) to his invention of a machine designed to exhibit paintings in motion.

Architectons

A title given to the three-dimensional, abstract, architectural forms of Malevich (1878-1935). See Constructivism.

Architectural Art

A term coined in the 1980s to reflect the integration of carefully crafted, site-specific art — often made of tile, wood, plaster, glass, or other material — into a building. See Mosaic and Stained Glass.

Architecture

- The art or science of designing and building structures.
- The art of shaping space to meet human needs.
- The bone structure of a city.

See Deconstruction and Visionary Architecture.

Armory Show (1913)

A well-known international exhibition given in New York City to show "the works of progressive and live painters, both American and foreign." The works of Delacroix, Duchamp, Goya, Ingres, van Gogh, and many others were shown along with those of American artists. After the exhibition was described as "lurid and degenerate," the general feeling was that "American art will never be the same again." In all, it had a strong effect on the viewing public. See Modern Art.

Artagraphy (1990s)

A new process in which reproductions of original paintings look and feel like original oils. Basic steps involve creating a bas-relief mold of the original, using a silicon-based material which is poured directly onto the canvas. (For older works, the artist re-creates the brushwork; this copy is used to create the mold.) Then the original is scanned with a laser that can differentiate up to 35,000 colors. This information is digitized and used to create seven or eight color separations. Finally, the laser image is placed on top of the mold, which is then placed on top of a canvas. This is heated to about 500 degrees F. and placed under 40 tons of pressure. By A.R.T., Inc., of Ontario. See Repligraphy.

Art and its various definitions

1. A method of instruction through delight. (Greek)
2. That which instructs, arouses pious emotions and awakens memories. (St. Bonaventura)

3. Painting is a science and should be pursued as an enquiry into the laws of Nature. (Constable)
4. . . . the outward expression of an inner need. (Kandinsky)
5. . . . exactitude winged by intuition. (Klee)
6. A picture . . . is essentially a flat surface covered with colors assembled in a certain order. (Denis)
7. There is no such thing as art. There are only artists. (Gombrich)
8. Organized perception is what art is all about. (Lichtenstein)

Art & Language

An Anglo-American association which came into being in 1968. The artists were convinced that art must, first and foremost, be information. They wanted to investigate the language of art in print, tape, film, photography, and posters. "Conversation, discussion, and conceptualism" were their motifs. In later years, however, they became less anti-visual. See Word-Art.

(ART)^n (1990s)

A team of artists and scientists who use computerized equipment to produce art they call "Phscologram": a light-box-mounted transparency that projects something like the three dimensionality seen in holograms. In tilting one's head, side views of the object are seen: a brightly lit hallucination within a dark, indefinite space. The philosophy of the enterprise is that invisible, unexplored worlds may become visible: images produced exist only as theoretical entities.

Art Appraisal

Several of its criteria are rarity, fame, aesthetic value, and condition of the artwork.

Art Brut (raw art)

A term coined by Dubuffet (1901-1985) to describe creations of the insane and the eccentric, as well as of derelicts, prisoners, and other marginal figures.

The artist's own work was inspired by primitive and children's art. It appears in small-scale productions such as paintings, drawings, and sculptures and in architectural renderings of surreal-like temples, tombs, and labyrinths. See Outsider Art.

Art Consultant

A person with a solid art background who is retained, usually by a large corporation, to give advice on art purchases. The educational process begins with a slide presentation and may extend to gallery or studio visits. The consultant must be aware of artistic preferences of both executives and employees.

Art Critic

One who is engaged in the observation, analysis, interpretation, and evaluation of art. It involves knowledge of the liberal arts. Important roles played by the critic are to recognize new artistic developments and to generally inform the public about art.

As a practical profession, art criticism is relatively new: its beginnings can be traced to the mid-1800s. Chas. F. Baudelaire (1821-1867) has been referred to as the father of contemporary art criticism. He challenged artists to capture the spectacle of life in the modern city; his writings had an enduring influence on the first modernists.

Art Dealer (recently called "gallerist")

The main function of the art dealer is to represent the art world in the marketplace. Besides acting as a trader, the art dealer needs a thorough knowledge of the whole range of art and must be able to (1) distinguish between good and bad art, (2) spot new talent, and (3) know the tastes of clients in order to offer them the right artworks for their collections.

Because of personal integrity and foresight, many dealers have earned national or international fame, most notably Paul Durand-Ruel (1831-1921), Charles Daniel (1878-1971), D.H. Kahnweiler (1884-1979), and Leo Castelli (1907-   ).

The art market as the Greeks and Romans knew it, and as we know it today, did not begin to thrive until the years of the Early Renaissance.

Art Deco (1920s-1930s)

An international, decorative style marked by a modern, streamlined look and bold, rhythmic, geometric arrangements such as spirals, zigzags, and ovals. Objects adapted to Art Deco include glasswork, pottery, porcelain, fashion and accessories, prints and posters, metalwork and jewelry, furniture and textiles, plastics, sculpture, and architecture.

It was a luxurious, high style that reflected attitudes of life, love, and money.

The Chrysler Building, the Empire State Building, and Rockefeller Center in New York City and more than 400 buildings, including the post office, in an area called the Deco District in Miami Beach are classic of its architecture. The liner *Normandie* was the last great expression of French Art Deco.

Currently, Art Deco seems to be making a small comeback.

Art Engagé/Arte Comprometido

Referring to art with political or social meaning. See Revolutionary Art.

Arte Povera (poor art)

A term coined by the critic G. Celant in 1967 when Italian artists explored territories beyond the traditional: art as life and art of the everyday juxtaposed with the question of what art was or could be.

Essentially, it embodies the creation of art from rough and worthless materials or from common environmental matter to create a mood or poetic feeling: estrangement from the natural world is brought into focus. Its major approaches:

1. Trash, scrap materials, fabric, and stones adapted in the creation of poetic assemblages.
2. Nature replicated in the form of fake forests, rocky sculptures, and igloos.

Artex International Fine Art Exchange

A market promoted as "the world's first computer fine arts sales system — serving both sellers and buyers." Constantly updated, with pictures of artworks scanned from auction catalogs every day, the system is designed to meet professional needs: buyers can browse, using any combination of criteria. When a selection is made, the purchaser makes an offer and transmits funds to a bank. The artwork is then shipped to the member gallery for approval and acceptance by the buyer.

"Art for Art's Sake"

Forms, colors, lines, and space are arranged for their own sake rather than for the illustration of man, nature, or history, or to serve any cultural or social establishments.

Art Form

A recognized form of artistic expression.

Art Gallery

1. A place where artworks are sold for profit. The principal activity of the owner is to establish the importance of artists chosen and represented by the gallery and to inspire the confidence of collectors to purchase the art. The first commercial art gallery in the US is believed to have been J.J. Gillespie; it opened in Pittsburgh in 1832. In 1849, Düsseldorf Gallery opened in New York. See Artex International Fine Art Exchange.
2. A room or building dedicated to the exhibition of artworks. In 1811, Rembrandt Peale (1778-1860) opened the Apollodorian Gallery — the first privately owned exhibition gallery in the US devoted exclusively to the fine arts. See Micro Galleries and Museum.

Artguard

A pen-and-ink system that uses DNA imprints to "sign" artworks with an identification code that cannot be altered. The inventor Chas. Butland claims his invention will reduce art theft and help resolve issues of provenance.

Art History

Concerning a lifetime of learning in the liberal arts. It offers a rich and varied knowledge and broadens the experience of those who perceive it. It includes the study of artworks in their historical origins and settings, enabling art appreciators to understand how painters and sculptors responded to different situations.

Giorgio Vasari, a 16th-century Italian architect, painter, and decorator, has often been called the first art historian.

Articulation

The manner in which adjacent shapes or forms join — a technique that varies with each painter.

Artifact

A simple object showing workmanship, particularly referring to a product of human activity/progress, a specific culture, or a period in history. The oldest known artifact is a stone tool, among other items, from Tanzania dating from 1.6 million B.C.

Art Informel (art without form; free abstraction) (1940s-1950s)

An important European (especially Spanish) school after WWII, which corresponded with the New York School in the use of cryptic symbols and unconscious calligraphy (automatism). It was a spontaneous, subjective, and gestural form of Abstract art that gave expression to the fantasy of an "obscure half world." Occasionally, it was referred to as "un art autre" (another art). Its major approaches: Expressive Abstraction, Tachisme, and Lyrical Abstraction. See El Paso, Gutai Group, and Zen.

Artisan

A craftsperson or one who possesses manual dexterity and skill.

Artists' Books

See Bookworks.

Artist's Proof or A/P

One or more proofs of a limited edition of prints. They are made for the artist's use for specific purposes such as correction or addition. Signed but unnumbered proofs are occasionally sold.

Art Jewelry

The concept of jewelry as art is manifested in the work of many fine artists and craftspersons who create unique pieces for expressive purposes. Although artistically designed jewelry is an old tradition, the combination of new and old materials, together with graphic imagery, has resulted in a new art form in which no distinction is made between artist and jeweler.

Art Mobilier

Small movable artworks, especially the carvings and decorated pieces found on prehistoric sites and the artifacts made by nomadic tribes.

Art Movement

An informal group of artists who work together for practical, as well as ideological, purposes. In some instances, they have shared workshops and materials and published periodicals or books. Movements usually last no longer than five years because members leave to form other groups or they change their style. At times, artists will be designated as belonging to a certain movement based on the timing of their recognition.

Art Nouveau (1890s-1914)

An international luxury style in design emerging from the Symbolist movement. It was marked by curvilinear pattern and flowing line and generally applied to interior decoration. Designers were occupied largely with the minor arts: art glasswork, book illustration, furniture, tapestries, and wallpaper. Architecture inspired by Art Nouveau patterns can be seen in many structures in major European cities.

The principal American working in full Art Nouveau style was Tiffany (1848-1933) whose lamps, stained-glass windows, and vases are highly prized. Tiffany achieved special effects by working color and texture into his stained-glass pieces while the glass was still hot. His creations resulted in the production of some of the greatest glassworks ever seen. See Decorative Arts and Glass Sculpture.

Art of Denunciation

A term coined by the Brazilian art world to describe the photographic images and sculptures produced by Krajcberg (1921-   ) in denunciation of the destruction of forests by fires deliberately set by Brazilian farmers and ranchers. The artist calls his images of charred tree trunks, roots, and vines "skeletons from the forest."

Art Patron

A wealthy or influential supporter of an artist or of the fine arts. During centuries past, it was common for the Catholic Church, royalty, and the aristocracy to support artists and to commission and purchase artworks.

One of the most famous patrons of the arts was Lorenzo the Magnificent of the Medici family. His most notable beneficiary was the boy Michelangelo; Leonardo da Vinci was another recipient of his patronage. (As a note to history, from 1400 to 1743, members of the Medici family were the most illustrious patrons of art, of learning, and of science in modern history.)

Art Period

A specific age which produces art possessing similar characteristics. An artist usually expresses the time in which he lives. The major divisions are (1) ancient, noted for sculpture, (2) medieval, noted for architecture, and (3) modern, noted for painting.

Art Photography

1. In the words of M. McKenzie: In the hands of a great photographer, a camera becomes a precise and sensitive instrument for rendering shape and light, shade and form, into pictures that can move us as dramatically as any art form. The power within the truth of this statement is exemplified by the masterpieces of photography's first 150 years. The integration of photography into the other arts considered fine is both ongoing and historically interesting.
2. In a historical sense, re-creation through photography has revealed some singular works. Lost to the world because of isolation (private ownership, the underground vault, the sanctuary, the facade of the temple, the tomb, or the sacred grotto), many artworks, including magnificent creations in the minor arts, have become well known through the medium of photography.
3. Because it has been recognized that photography relates as much to popular culture as it does to high art, art museums have been in the process of finding their own photographic expression with the work of such well-known photographers as Ansel Adams, Richard Avedon, Bill Brandt, Jan Groover, Richard Prince, Cindy Sherman, and many others. The Museum of Modern Art in Manhattan is recognized as the first major art museum to take photography seriously as art by establishing a regular program of collecting and exhibiting photographs: Steichen (1879-1973) was director of the photography department from 1947 to 1962. His most popular exhibition

was "The Family of Man" (1955) which included the work of 273 photographers from 68 countries; its theme was to reveal the essential oneness of humankind.

Arts and Crafts Movement (1875-1920)

An English but eventually international, reactionary movement against the standardizing effects of the machine and mass production, inspired by Wm. Morris (1834-1896), a writer and designer. A call was made for the return to handcraftsmanship and simplicity along with the plea of "joy in labor." It emphasized the need for integrating beauty into everyday life and encouraged the return of the artistic craftsmanship that marked the Middle Ages. In the US, the call was so strong that communities and societies were established and books and magazines published to promote a back-to-basics philosophy in design.

In sum, the movement fostered individual creativity by elevating the status of the production process in what has been called "the union of hand, head and heart in handicraft": the way things were made was as important as their appearance. Design appropriate to intended use, artistic merit, and historical importance were relevant to the creation of pottery, ceramic tiles, furniture, wood carvings, graphics, textiles, printing, bookbinding, and silver and copper objects.

Art Preservation Law

Currently, there are 11 states in the US that give artists some rights to their creations after an artwork has been sold: if works are altered, removed, or destroyed, the artist may gain the right to sue for damages.

Art Students League of New York

A school organized in 1875 for the purpose of teaching sketching, drawing, and painting. It has no set course of study. It has enjoyed success through the years and has attracted many distinguished teachers to its staff. A great many former students have become well-known artists.

Arts-Watch International

An organization comprised of professional people in the arts, as well as poets, writers, and musicians, whose principal activity is to keep an eye on restoration work. Its bill of rights has been set up to protect major works from excessive restoration: whenever possible, artworks should remain in their original abode and, when necessary, only the blandest techniques are to be used in restoring them.

Art Theory

The discussion and establishment of philosophical standards concerning the purpose of art.

Art Therapy

A free form of art used to relieve patients of stress. See Outsider Art.

Ash Can School (1897-1917)

The first American movement of the 20th century, comprising five American Realist painters (Glackens, Henri, Luks, Shinn, and Sloan) who had exhibited with and were part of The Eight. Social commentary on the realities of life in the urban world was their theme; these pictures constitute a panorama of the erupting metropolis. Their representations of people, streets, theater, restaurants, nightlife, etc., depicting both the lowlife and the highlife, made them seem radical to the established world. Many regarded their work "as a deliberate conspiracy to blacken the eye of America . . . with impolite aspects of life." Some called them the "Apostles of Ugliness"; they have been more accurately called the "New York Realists." See American Realism and 14th Street School.

Assemblage

A term coined by the artist Dubuffet to describe the integration of art with ready-mades or found objects: an art form that exists somewhere between painting and sculpture. The magical and expressive possibilities of the medium lie in the artist's ability to combine and assemble disparate or unrelated elements.

Atelier

1. The workshop of an artist or craftsperson.
2. A studio where an artist trains students or where assistants work under the artist's supervision.
3. During the Middle Ages, construction of large churches and cathedrals was directed by the master architect and the master of the works. Under the leadership of the master architect, an atelier was set up. Upon completion of the project, it was moved to another site; this enabled artistic and architectural ideas to be spread throughout major areas of Europe.
4. A print workshop that offers an artist the facilities, equipment, and technical assistance for creating and printing graphic works. See Printmaking.

Athenaeum, The

The world-renowned portrait of George Washington by Stuart (1755-1828). Copies of this portrait were made by many hands, including the artist's daughter, Jane Stuart (1812-1888).

Stuart developed a distinctive style when he concentrated on the sitter's head only: timeless impressions were made with the elimination of costume and setting. His work had a wide and permanent effect on portrait-making in the US. See Portrait d'Apparat.

Attribute

A conventional, symbolic object used for identifying a meaning such as a dog for fidelity or the scales of Justice. Also, an object associated with a person, often a saint in an artwork, and shown as his/her "sign." For example, St. Catherine's wheel.

Attribution, Attributed to

The assignment of an artwork to a certain artist or school based on style or documentary evidence. See Deattribution.

Audio Installation Art

The use of computer and audio technology within a tableau or setting where the interaction between the atmosphere and the environment becomes "visible": a sophisticated kinetic sculpture transformed into sound through a physical act such as touch or movement. See Multimedia, Tableaux Éclatés, and Video Art.

Audiokinetic Sculpture

A sculpture or construction in which lights, sounds, music, movement, labyrinths, and mirrors are combined to give the effect of a sculpture funhouse. See Groupe de Recherche.

Auto-Iconography

The use by artists of surreal images, symbols, allusions, disguises, autobiographical elements, myth, and legend, with iconographical self-portraiture as the motif: from portrait to portrait the artist composes variations on the same theme. Classic is the work of two Mexican artists: Kahlo (1907-1954) and Zenil (1947-).

Automatic Drawing

A technique practiced by Kelly (1923-) in which he allowed ink to run down a page and then guided it by blowing on the ink. He wanted to get rid of preconceived ideas about art.

Automatism

This technique is central to the theme of Surrealism. The expression of deep and basic emotions is seen in the form of a spontaneous sketch: free association and intuition release subconscious imagery. Picasso used the phrase "voyage of discovery."

Automatistes, Les (1946-1951)

A term coined by the critic Marsil in 1947 to describe a group of seven Montreal artists who were influenced by the techniques of Surrealism, especially automatism.

Autoportrait

The exploration of the work of contemporary artists who use video to investigate the self.

Avant-Garde (advance guard: "ahead of the times")

An intellectual group that develops unconventional or experimental concepts. The artist is a precursor to future art, in contrast to traditional concentration on the past.

Aviation and Space Art

The creation of paintings depicting the age of flight and space travel. Many of the images have been recorded by the aviators and astronauts themselves. Artists of this genre have realistically portrayed man's visual experience with the universe, as well as the history of early flights, technological advances, and the conquest of space. Famous air battles have also been recorded.

B

Bambocciate (1630s-late 1600s)

These small paintings, produced by Northern European artists working in Rome, often portrayed people of low social status as picturesque or ridiculous. (The artists were called "Bamboccianti.")

Barbarian Art

The term "barbarian" was applied by Greeks and Romans to persons outside their own culture. The art of wandering tribes in Europe, Asia, and Africa was diverse and lively with a sense of beauty and much skill. Endemic to nomadic living was the decoration of tents, weapons, jewelry, and metalwork. Their strong feelings for design and bright colors influenced the medieval arts of sculpture, architecture, and manuscript painting.

Barbizon School (1830s-1870s)

A group of French artists who broke with the tradition of depicting human figuration when they began to portray the countryside. The artists transformed Western landscape painting: they were among the first to recognize and capture the changing colors of the seasons and the effect of light playing on the landscape. The forest of Fontainebleau was the subject of many works. Another popular theme was the activity of peasants.

Corot (1796-1875)
Troyon (1810-1865)
T. Rousseau (1812-1867)
Millet (1814-1875)
Daubigny (1817-1878)

See Macchiaioli School.

Baroque (1590-1730)

A style of painting, sculpture, and architecture born in Rome. Although it took on diverse forms in several countries, it was the predominant style in Europe of that time. Baroque was a direct outgrowth of Mannerism, and is characterized by excessive light/shade, rich ornamentation, emotionalism, illusion, and an increased use of color. Essentially, Baroque produced scenarios in which drama was presented within the forms of painting, sculpture, and architecture.

Bernini (1598-1680), a sculptor and architect, is recognized as its dominant force. He worked on various projects at St. Peter's for over 40 years; his *Ecstasy of St. Teresa* is classic of Baroque sculpture.

Rubens (1577-1640), a Flemish painter, caused its popularity to grow on an international scale. He was the first artist to develop Baroque movement. By the 1600s, the Netherlands had split into two religious groups. In the Northern Protestant part, art became restricted to non-religious subjects such as portraiture, still life, marine painting, and landscape. (Those artists who were not portraitists could no longer depend on commissions but, instead, painted pictures in the hope of attracting buyers.) It was discovered at this time that great paintings could be created from commonplace subject matter, especially in still life: flower painting was a popular genre.

French Baroque (also called Baroque Classicism) was reflected mainly in architecture. During the Age of Versailles, Paris replaced Rome as the center of pictorial arts. Spanish Baroque is seen mostly in portraiture and religious themes.

In sum, paintings of the 1600s, with many themes taken from history, mythology, and allegory, have been divided into several categories:

—Classicism (Renaissance influence: technical mastery and idealized treatment).

—Naturalism/Realism (a popular style of the Dutch School; subjects were drawn from everyday life, including landscapes and interiors).

—Academic Classicism (formal and technically correct).

—High Baroque (the work of Rubens is classic: concern for the entire composition, dynamic and dramatic effect, extravagant form). See Rococo.

Bateau-Lavoir Group

A discussion group consisting of the first followers of Cubism in Paris. See Puteaux Group.

Bauhaus (1919-1933)

A school formed by Gropius (1883-1969) in Germany to combine art and design and to develop a creative approach in architecture, painting, metalwork, ceramics, photography, advertising, typography, furniture design, and, especially, industrial mass production. In essence, it attempted to dissolve all distinctions between the fine and applied arts and to come up with a new approach to teaching art.

The Bauhaus became a symbol for creative construction and revolutionized the practice of art and design. "Form follows function" was its motto. Its influence on industrial design was profound; Bauhaus products became prototypes for mass-produced items. (Many of the utensils and furnishings seen and used today are tributes to Bauhaus design.)

In nearly every American and European city there are buildings designed in the clean style that Bauhaus architects pioneered.

Staff members were Albers, Klee, and Kandinsky in the fine arts; Bayer in graphics; Moholy-Nagy in photography; Schlemmer in theater; and Gropius, van der Rohe, and Meyer in architecture.

When the school was closed by the Nazis in 1933, many of its teachers immigrated to the US and re-established a school in Chicago in 1937.

In 1976, East German rulers decided to revive Bauhaus functionalism and modernism. By 1987, the Bauhaus Center in Dessau began shaping itself into a think tank, a research center, and an experimental school concentrating on environmental/ecological problems. In 1995, Bauhaus Museum opened in Weimar. Its aim is to "create a spirited dialog between the avant-garde of the 1920s and contemporary trends in art and society."

Baxter Prints

A printing process perfected by Baxter (1804-1867), whose reproductions were noted for their color, perspective, and accuracy. They were quite comparable to oil paintings.

Bay Area Figuration (sometimes called Realist Expressionism) (1955-1965)

The painters in this group shared several overall characteristics: contemporary subject matter (portraiture, landscape and still life); loose brushwork; brilliant light; and saturated color. Classic is the work of Diebenkorn (1922-1993). See *Ocean Park.*

Bayeux Tapestry

A 230-foot-long strip of wool supported by cloth, with 72 embroidered scenes depicting the Norman Conquest of England in 1066, with emphasis on battles, bloodshed, and feasting, commingled with scenes from everyday life: a picture-chronicle. It is thought to have been made in England by teams of embroiderers and then shipped to Bayeux. This tapestry has been called "the most important monument of secular art of the Middle Ages" during the Romanesque period.

Bella Maniera

The highest expression of an age. See Grand Manner.

Belle Peinture

1. The tradition of an artist whose pleasure lies in the craft, material, and technique of painting.
2. A highly accomplished type of painting that employs all the painting skills.

Bergeries

Pictures of landscape, similar to pastorals, in which people are portrayed as simple country folk although, in reality, they are not. This style was popular in England and France during the 1700s. See Fêtes Galantes.

Berlin Wall Art Collection

When the Berlin Wall was destroyed, some 170 tons of it were preserved so that painters and sculptors might use the unusual surface to create artworks.

Biedermeir Style (1815-1848)

Known mainly as a furniture style in Austria and Germany (c. 1800-1860). In painting, it was popular in Austria, Denmark, Germany, and Switzerland, with Realism as its essence in the depiction of landscapes, genre scenes, and still lifes. Serenity, order, and restraint characterized the times.

Biennial Exhibition of Contemporary American Painting (also called the Corcoran Biennial)

Hailed as the oldest continuous biennial in the US, with its beginnings in 1907, it is also the only exhibition that focuses exclusively on painting.

Bildarchitektur (pictorial architecture)

A term coined by Kassak (1887-1967), an important figure in the Central European avant-garde movement. It was his theory that Bildarchitektur was a symbol of action: that nonobjective art was to become a political statement without relaying any story. Geometric form and pure color, according to Kassak, were signs of truth.

Biomorphic Abstraction

A form suggesting a living organism, in contrast to geometric or lifeless form. Biomorphism is traced to the first abstract relief sculpture of Arp (1887-1966) created in 1916: a wood study of soft organic shapes. This technique was eventually adopted as a motif by designers and architects between 1930 and 1955. (The term, however, has now come to be used for all periods of art, from prehistoric to modern.)

Bird's-Eye View

A scene depicted as though observed far above it, especially suitable for panoramas. Classic is *The Midnight Ride of Paul Revere* by Wood (1892-1942); topographical and architectural views are seen in detail from a height. More recently, Jacquette (1934-) has painted landscapes as viewed from the air.

Birds of America, The

Wilson (1766-1813) produced eight volumes of his *American Ornithology*, both illustrations and text, which evidence a poet's feeling for both language and nature.

Audubon (1785-1851) produced a double-elephant folio depicting, in life-size, *The Birds of America, from Original Drawings with 435 Plates Showing 1,065 Figures*, published in four volumes, along with *Ornithological Biography*. Audubon succeeded in creating beauty and drama with precise and graceful renderings of birds.

These publications were regarded as achievements without equal.

Black American Art

Generally, black American art relates to (1) the black experience in the US, from Colonial days to the Harlem Renaissance to the black power movement of recent decades, (2) the rejection of Europeanism in favor of the motifs, symbols, and colors of Africa, and (3) the rendering of artworks that reflect the interests and sensibilities of black Americans.

In sum, historical and political concerns and events, memory, ceremony, spirituality, myth, and folklore play important roles in black American art. The artists, each one unique, are nevertheless united by a common desire to reveal a shared history and tradition.

Well-known artists include:

- Johnson (a/k/a/ Johnston) (active 1796-1824) A self-taught artist who was the first black American portrait painter in the US and the first to gain recognition during his own lifetime. He was a portraitist of Maryland's prosperous merchants and planters.
- Duncanson (1822-1872) His oeuvre consists of romantic landscapes, portraiture, genre scenes, and still lifes. By the 1860s, the artist was regarded as "the best landscape painter in the West." He was one of the first black artists to attain an international reputation and to make a living as a painter.
- Bannister (1828-1901) His standing in New England was high. He depicted harmonious and spiritual landscapes as an expression of his religious beliefs.

The artist became the first African American to receive a national award.

- Lewis (1843-1890) A popular sculptor who was the first black American to win international fame. She re-created figures from history and literature and was particularly interested in exploring universal human rights issues, especially when depicting black American and native American women who had struggled and suffered.
- Traylor (1855-1947) An illiterate farmer whose period of artistic activity from 1939 to 1942 produced about 1500 drawings. He favored the depiction of domestic animals and is known primarily as a folk artist.
- Tanner (1859-1937) He studied with Eakins and was an inspiration to other black American artists during his lifetime, setting an example for generations of artists. His milieu was genre scenes, landscapes and, particularly, religious themes. His draftsmanship was in the academic tradition.
- Scott (1884-1964) His canvases include colorful depictions of Haitian life, studies of black Americans, and genre scenes. He was one of the first black painters to discard Europeanism.
- Jackson, M. (1887-1931) A pioneer in the depiction of black subjects. She is known for her portrait busts of African American culture.
- Waring (1887-1948) She is known for portraiture, as well as for genre scenes depicting African American life.
- Johnson (1887-1967) As a sculptor, he was committed to "producing strictly a Negro art . . . aiming to show the natural beauty and dignity . . . as to the Negro himself."
- Pippin (1888-1946) His work is characterized by a decorative but sophisticated, primitive style. He painted everyday scenes, still lifes, historic events, biblical narrative, and his recollections of childhood and war experiences. Pippin was known for his graphic work for publications and established himself as a master of color and design.
- Thomas (1891-1978) Her mosaic-like, abstract paintings were executed in lavish, vibrant color. She was inspired by the world around her, especially flowers.
- Motley (1891-1981) Known for his dignified, academic portraits of black figures, for paintings of life in East Africa, and for humorous, genre scenes of life in Chicago, including a host of neighborhood characters. He was one of the first black Americans to have a one-man exhibition in the US.
- Pierce (1892-1984) As a woodcarver in the Folk art tradition, he was influenced by autobiographical elements, spiritual beliefs, moralizing themes, the print media, and black celebrities.
- Evans (1892-1987) A folk artist whose vividly, almost psychedelically, colored art was often inspired by dreams and religious visions, with emphasis on floral, human, animal, and mythical figuration. She often used whatever materials were on hand: scrap paper, window shades, bookbindings, etc.
- Douglas (1898-1979) He was called the father of black art in his role as an exponent of black iconography in contemporary art, especially as seen in symbolic representations of historical and cultural memories.
- Savage (1900-1962) She became the nation's youngest known sculptor, as well as a teacher and spokesperson for black artists.

- Woodruff (1900-1980) His early murals of black history are best known. In later years, he painted in an abstract style, often incorporating black imagery into his work.
- Johnson (1901-1970) He painted images of black life, incorporating the imagery of his heritage and childhood into a Naive art which is recognized as unique in its expression of black culture.
- Barté (1901-1988) A sculptor known for his realistic portrayals of religious subjects, figures from black history, and stage and dance celebrities.
- Porter (1905-1970) He is most remembered for his skill as a portraitist and a book illustrator.
- Bearden (1914-1988) His vivid, kaleidoscopic paper collages are imaginative and expressive of the life and experience of black Americans, especially as seen in street scenes and in the South.
- Lawrence (1917-) His work is imbued with concern for social issues and historic events affecting black Americans. He was a pioneer in illustrating the struggle of his people for equal rights and in depicting ghetto life. Classic are narrative paintings titled *The Migration Series* and *Life in Harlem*.
- Biggers (1924-) He portrays the spiritual beauty of black Americans in fields, farmlands, and in nature.
- Colescott (1925-) He is known for his biting humor in reworked themes of famous paintings—van Gogh's *Potato Eaters* became *Eat Dem Taters* — as well as for the reworking of Old Masters.
- Saar (1926-) An assemblage artist who works with found objects: bits of glass, colored wire, and melted metal are the materials of small, metaphysical artworks. Her re-creations of white culture's stereotypic images of black Americans are represented in provocative collages and constructions: *The Liberation of Aunt Jemima* portrays Aunt Jemima holding a pistol and a rifle.
- Dial (1928-) A self-taught artist whose large-scale, assemblage-paintings, embedded with found wood, metal, wire, rope, and other industrial materials, convey themes of the Africans' entry into the New World, the Civil Rights movement, and the economic/social condition of black Americans. Titles of works reflect the artist's social commentary such as *Everybody Got a Right to the Tree of Life* and *AIDS: Freedom Ain't Free.*
- Ringgold (1930-) As a painter and sculptor, she has rendered many works based on social/political life: the Civil Rights era, the Black Nationalist movement, feminism, etc. The African influence is seen in her slave-trade series *Slave Rape*. Best known are her quilts composed of painted and dyed fabrics intertwined with written narrative and painted imagery, especially a series titled *The Woman on the Bridge*. See Soft Sculpture.
- Edwards (1937-) A sculptor whose iconography is provocative. There are over 100 pieces in his series *Lynch Fragments* which he has created since 1963. They include objects identified with the labor of and the violence to slaves.
- Chase-Riboud (1939-) Influenced by Egyptian culture, many of her creations combine bronze and textile ropes which resemble human figuration.
- Birch (1942-) A figurative artist known for brightly colored papier-mâché busts and for large gouache paper paintings that are framed in papier-mâché. The artist's themes are black pride, racial bigotry, the Civil Rights movement, everyday life, and social situations.

- Brown (1945-) He is known for dramatic but distorted portraits of artists and musicians, scenes from urban life and lore, and religious motifs.
- Bailey (1967-) His assemblages center around old photos from his own family and from black American history, set amid brightly colored backgrounds.

Black Paintings

A term used by Goya (1746-1828) to describe his paintings which concentrate on death, destruction, and cruelty. He thought the task of art was to cry out the anguish of man forsaken by God. Goya's work is thought to have foreshadowed or prefigured all Modern art. See Capriccios.

Blackware

Beginning in early 20th-century New Mexico, Pueblo Indians developed a distinctive black-on-black technique of pottery making.

Blue Period

A short period (c. 1901-1904) during the life of Picasso (1881-1973) when he used monochromatic blue or blue/green in the depiction of society's rejects, the poor, the lonely, and the defeated: anguish, sadness, desolation, and resignation to life's sorrows are reflected.

The Rose period (c. 1905-1906) was a time when the artist's thoughts were changing and he abandoned the gloom of prior years. He started to paint a number of subjects in several styles; circus performers were a favorite subject. Coloration was suffused with rose hues.

Blue Rider, The (Der Blaue Reiter) (1911-1914)

Another German Expressionist group with Kandinsky (1866-1944) and Marc (1880-1916) as its exponents. They published the almanac *Der Blaue Reiter* which contained articles on the fine arts, music, theater, and reproductions of diverse art forms from several countries and from other ages. The group's aim was to demonstrate the qualities of artistic expression and to liberate artists from traditional restrictions. The artists wanted to show what was essential in art when they used visual symbols and unrealistic, expressive color to convey strong emotion. Their primitive-like style was used for the depiction of forms from nature and the beauty of the world, including scenes from urban life.

Jawlensky (1864-1941)
Feininger (1871-1956)
Münter (1877-1962)
Klee (1879-1940)
Macke (1887-1914)

See November Group.

Bodegón (still life)

A term referring to the juxtaposition of the sacred and the secular—a genre of painting popular in Spain during the 1600s. Classic is *Kitchen Maid With the Supper at Emmaus* by Velásquez (1599-1660).

Body Art

A term that has been applied to both Performance art and to the fashion of body modification through tattooing, piercing, and scarification/sculpture.

Bolognese School

L. Carracci (1555-1619)
Agostino Carracci (1557-1602)
Annibale Carracci (1560-1609)
Mastelletta 1575-1655)
Cavedone (1577-1660)
Tiarini (1577-1668)
Domenichino (1581-1641)

Bon-á-tirer (good-to-pull)

The impression selected by the artist as a guide for pulling the entire edition. It provides a standard of quality against which all other impressions are compared. See Print and Printmaking.

Book of Hours

A religious book offering prayers and meditations appropriate to each hour, day, or month. This book and other religious books were sometimes commissioned as engagement or wedding gifts. See *Trés Riches Heures*.

Book of Kells, The

A manuscript of the gospels, written in Latin, dating from the 8th/9th centuries, located in Dublin. It is classic of manuscript illumination and is regarded as a landmark in the spread of Christian art and religion.

Bookworks or Artists' Books

During the recent past, contemporary artists have revived a centuries-old style of artistic expression: pages, containing unusual typography and imagery, are folded, molded, densely layered, sculptured, or otherwise re-formed, to present unique artists' books that may be either one-of-a-kind or produced in small, limited editions. Many of the bookworks have sold for thousands of dollars.

Border Art

In recent efforts to make vibrant, cross-border cultural exchanges, artists in both Mexico and the US have explored a range of complex personal and political issues raised by the border's presence.

Bottega (workshop)

Commonly referring to the studio or workroom of an artist, especially the area where apprentices or assistants work. Classic are the workshops of Renaissance painters who were busy for much of the time in the production of objects other than paintings and sculptures, such as plates, chests, and beds. See Atelier.

Bozzetto

Referring to the sketch or model for a painting or sculpture. See Maquette.

Brandywine Tradition/School

A photographically realistic style promoted by the illustrator Pyle (1853-1911) in the late 1800s. He taught and influenced many illustrators, most notably N. C. Wyeth (1882-1945), whose family members and students further advanced this technique. A museum has been established in Chadds Ford, Pennsylvania, to permanently house the works of the Wyeth family, generally regarded as the first family of American art today. See Illustrator and Peale Family.

Bravura

A term meaning bravery or skill, used in art to describe technical virtuosity, often implying daring and vigorous brushwork.

Bridge, The (Die Brücke) (1905-1913)

Because they hated the cruel social caste in Germany, a group of four university students formed the first Expressionist movement to protest conditions and to effect a change. The artists wanted to capture the essence of reality in form and color. Paintings, characterized by strident color and a coarsening of technique, have as common subject matter scenes from urban life, social/political messages, landscapes, nude portraiture, and religion, all expressive of passion and emotion in an attempt to arrive at the basis of human character.

Woodcuts for the wide dissemination of prints became a popular medium. Although the artists proclaimed a kinship with German art of the 1500s, they regarded their work as "a bridge to the future."

Gallen-Kallela (1865-1931)
Nolde (1867-1956)
Müller (1874-1930)
Kirchner (1880-1938)
Bleyl (1880-1966)
Pechstein (1881-1955)
Heckel (1883-1970)
Schmidt-Rottluff (1884-1976)

See Blue Rider and New Artists' Association.

Brown Sauce

A pejorative term used to describe the dark glazes of 19th-century paintings.

Brueghel Series (A Vanitas of Style)

A two-part, 80-panel work in which Steir (1939-) investigates the essence of style by assuming the hands of artists from the years of the High Renaissance through Abstract Expressionism.

Brushwork

A general term for the style in which paint is applied; it is regarded as an important aspect of the artist's "handwriting." See Signature Style.

Buckeye or Schlock Art

A disparaging term for stereotyped, mass-produced landscape paintings.

Butler Institute of American Art

Located in Youngstown, Ohio, this institute opened its doors in 1919 as the first museum in the US to show American art only.

Byzantine Art (A.D. 330-1453)

The development of art in Constantinople, which inherited its civilization from Rome, with the difference that in Byzantium the illusion of reality declined and two-dimensional flatness and stillness took precedence. This period includes the art produced in the Christian world when Western art became Byzantine in style. The more simple art of the Early Christian era was replaced by grandeur. Churches were built everywhere and decorated with mosaics — the chief decoration for a thousand years in Eastern churches.

Decorative sculpture, manuscript illumination, ivory carving, metalwork, and mosaics were the primary arts and crafts, with pictorial art represented in wall-and panel painting, all of which reached full expression in the 6th century during the reign of Justinian. In A.D. 726, Emperor Leo III declared that symbols of Christianity, rather than figurative art, were preferable. During this crisis, existing artworks were removed or destroyed. When the crisis ended A.D. 843, the Byzantine style continued.

Although the term "Byzantine" embraces a variety of painting styles, emphasis was on color effect, flat forms, and decorative highlights, with backgrounds of deep color or gold. See Carolingian Renaissance, Icon, and Romanesque.

C

Cabinet Painting

A term used to describe easel paintings in intimate surroundings, with particular reference to the genre and still-life scenes painted by the Little Masters of the Dutch School. It also refers to Spanish paintings of centuries past when artists treated minor events with great care and detail.

Hubbard (1807-1862) painted informal cabinet-size portraits (called "small whole length") on wood panels measuring 20" x 15" — a rarity in American portraiture. These near-miniaturist, carefully finished portraits incorporate backgrounds and personal accessories associated with the subject. Many likenesses are of celebrated Southern personages. See Portrait d'Apparat.

Calendar Art

Developed as an advertising tool in 1889, art calendars were popular because the reproductions of the work of American and European artists contained in the calendars were often the only artworks found in American homes during the late 1800s/early 1900s. Through the 20th century, no art form has been more widely available or more universally appreciated. Classic are the Brown & Bigelow calendar paintings by Rockwell (1894-1978).

California Impressionism

Because of its intense light, the ocean, the sky, and the climate, the landscape of California became the springboard for the work of many plein-air painters. Santa Barbara has been called "the first capital of California Impressionism" because of the pleasant ambiance found there and because of workshops dedicated to Impressionism.

Although this style declined with the advent of the Great Depression, during recent years Impressionism once again has found favor among artists, collectors, and museums, especially as rendered in paintings of California missions. See American Impressionism.

Calligrams

Conceived by the French writer Apollinaire, these shapes, patterns, and images are made entirely of letters. They are used for cards, stationery, posters, and advertising.

Calligraphy

The art of elegant handwriting; also, a very important art in the form of brushwork in China, Japan, and Islam. Calligraphy is also a traditional Jewish art form, with scribes writing Torah scrolls by hand on parchment. The Hebrew alphabet, the oldest still in use, has been called the most beautifully designed of all scripts.

In more recent years, calligraphy became a strong influence on several Abstract Expressionists. The modernist Marden (1938-   ) created a group of abstract paintings, titled *Cold Mountain*, based on Chinese calligraphy. See Shodo.

Calligraphy Drawings or Flourishings

An art form that evolved from the craze for excellent penmanship in the 1800s. Professional penmen and their students created lyrical images of farm scenes, animals, and birds. It is regarded as part of the American Folk art tradition.

Camden Town Group (1911-1913)

This small group of English painters, founded by Sickert (1860-1942), depicted scenes from contemporary life, cityscapes, landscapes, portraiture, and still lifes. It was one of the first groups of artists to be influenced by the work of the Post-Impressionists. Sickert wanted to change the course of English art. See The Eight.

Camera Obscura (room-size or hand-held)

A mechanical aid, sometimes referred to as a "magic box." It was used by Venetian and Dutch landscape artists to trace the visual relationship of size and shape in drawing from nature and the relationship between light and the visual image.

Canvas

A prepared cloth surface used for oil painting. The canvas was universally adopted, in place of wood panels, during Renaissance years.

Capriccios

1. A term used for paintings of real or imaginary landscapes, buildings, or architectural features in charming groupings. Classic is a series of six landscapes by Canaletto (1697-1768), titled *Lovelace Capriccios*, which depict quasi-English or Italianate landmarks.
2. Goya (1746-1828) used the title *Los Caprichos* for a series of 80 etchings in which he ridicules and satirizes society with contemptuous ferocity. See Black Paintings.

Caravaggisti

A term applied to painters of various backgrounds, who adopted the style of Caravaggio (1571-1610): realism and dramatic lighting. He was the first painter to spotlight his pictures like a stage director, contrasting brilliant highlights with sharply outlined, deep shadows. His ideas influenced all the important masters of Baroque painting. The work of LaTour (1593-1652) has been regarded as closest to the spirit of the great works of Carravaggio. See "Circle of."

Caricature

A comical, satirical, or grotesque rendering by means of distortion or exaggeration. The art of making people look ridiculous has influenced politics, society, and the arts for centuries. The term was first given its current meaning by Annibale Carracci of the Bolognese School, who applied it to his own drawings.

Carolingian Renaissance (A.D. 786-877)

Under the aegis of Charlemagne and Charles the Bald, the revival of art and literature was made possible through a reawakened interest in antiquity. Great works survived because Charlemagne built great monasteries where, for centuries to come, monks copied and preserved manuscripts of Greece, Rome, and Byzantium.

This period is especially known for covers produced for Bibles. Classic is the cover of the Lindau Gospels, made of jewels and gold, depicting the Crucified Christ as well as mourning angels and humans.

Illuminated manuscripts were also outstanding, most notably the Utrecht Psalter (Book of Psalms) created c. 832. See Illumination and Ottonian Renaissance.

Carousel Figures

Carved, polychromed animals and chariots for American carousels are now recognized as a significant expression of Folk art. Its history can be traced to 12th-century equestrian games in Asia Minor, later evolving into a widespread European sport. By the 1700s, wooden horses had replaced live ones.

Cartoon

1. In fine art, it refers to a full-scale preparatory drawing on heavy paper.
2. The drawing of comic strips or cartoons that have a message or story to convey beneath the surface, especially as in political satire. The first undisputed master of the comic strip and animated cartoon: W. McCay (1871-1934). More recently, Pop artists Lichtenstein (1925-1997), Warhol (1928-1987), and Ramos (1935-) made paintings of comic-book heroes. See Animation Art and Post-Pop Art.

In 1996 the International Museum of Cartoon Art was established in Boca Raton, Florida, where well-known cartoon characters are represented in a collection of more than 160,000 works.

Casein

The mixture of pigments with a granular powder derived from skim milk.

Casting

The process by which a sculpture may be reproduced from a model of wax or clay in a more durable material such as metal or plaster.

Catalogue Raisonné

1. The publication of a detailed or descriptive listing of an artist's work, which adds a measure of confidence to the marketability of the artworks.
2. A definitive listing of an artist's works, the whereabouts of such works, and their provenances.

Cave Art

Referring basically to Old Stone Age art discovered in Lascaux in Dordogne, France, in 1940 and in Altamira, Spain, in 1879. Generally, the figures depicted are animals, probably drawn or carved in the hope that the naturalistic representations, painted in red, black, and various ochres, would exert a certain magic realism: paintings and carvings were seen as actual re-creations, and it was believed that what man had copied he could control.

Paintings of animals and humans have also been discovered on numerous sites from Scandinavia to South Africa, most notably the outline drawings discovered in 1952 in a cave just outside Palermo. More recently, in 1994, an enormous underground cavern, containing more than 300 vivid images of animals, was discovered in Southern France. They have been dated at 30,000 years old.

Other Old Stone Age art is in the form of carvings on bone, horn, or stone. Female figures are known as Venuses. Middle Stone Age art is characterized by the painting of geometric designs on pebbles or rocks. New Stone Age art is characterized by wall paintings, weavings, pottery with geometric designs, and the erection of huge stones to mark burial grounds. (Many of the basic shapes of pottery known today were developed during this period.) See Aboriginal Art, Petroglyph, Pictograph, Prehistoric, and Primitive Art.

Ceramics

Referring to the art or technique of shaping and firing clay. Earthenware, porcelain, stoneware, tiles, and art pottery are the most common objects made.

Ceremonial Masks

For many centuries, cultures from around the world have created masks that represent animals, spirits, and other beings in rituals involving myth, mystery, and magic.

Certificate of Authenticity or C of A

A legal document that lists information relevant to the sale of a limited edition.

In the Native American culture, a certificate for newly created work provides the purchaser with proof that the work was created by an Indian of a particular tribe, is sold with the artist's permission, and is original work. See Indian Arts and Crafts Act.

Chance Configuration

Arp (1887-1966) was the first to cut shapes without thought and to arrange them according to chance. Duchamp (1887-1968) dropped threads on canvas and then traced them. Kelly (1923-) created compositions by tearing up drawings, dropping them at random, and then fixing them in place.

Chiaroscuro (bright/dark)

The dramatic use of light and shade and the contrast between them to create the illusion of depth and space. According to Leonardo da Vinci, it is "the true and natural arrangement of light and shade." See Tenebrism and Value.

Chiaroscuro in Nature

The creation of mood in landscape resulting from the play of light and shade. The American landscape artist Cole (1801-1848) said: "Light is the great stimulant. It is the fire of life."

Chicano Art

It is generally recognized as beginning in the 1960s with the Civil Rights and Chicano movements. A new form of aesthetics was born that defined the relationship between Mexican Americans and their Spanish culture. Poster art and murals were the most popular art forms. (The artworks of Los Tres Grandes were quite influential.) See Hispanic Art in the US.

Chinese Art

Over a period of 3500 years the art of China has remained quiet and conservative. Central to its theme is the expression of ideas and feelings, along with representations of nature.

During the early centuries, the ruling class created tombs of extraordinary size in which paintings and sculptures by the thousands were installed. Their burial chambers were similar to those of the Egyptians where vivid scenes were depicted.

Painting and calligraphy have been respected as the highest art forms for centuries. Poetry is intimately fused with painting: the poem inspires the artist. The crafts of ivory carving and lacquerwork were outstanding. Porcelain objects were highly prized. Bronze casting was known of c. 1700 B.C.

The calligraphic brushstroke has always been of prime importance. It has been the ambition of artists to acquire such ease with brush and ink so as to write a fresh vision immediately. Basically, paintings are marked by light and sketchy lines because of the materials and techniques used: light brush, wash, and black ink. The Chinese feel repetitive copying enhances personal technique.

Two schools evolved in the 16th/17th centuries. Painters in the Northern (academic) school became known for decoration and romantic realism; those of the Southern school became known for their grasp of the inner nature of things and high ideals.

After China opened its doors to Western trade, the calligraphic brushstroke was counterbalanced by bold colors, perspective, and chiaroscuro. As the old order of things collapsed, the desire for change and innovation became paramount. China's first art school, established in 1912, offered classes in both Western and Chinese style; figure painting, which had disappeared for almost a thousand years, made a strong comeback.

Thousands of art treasures were destroyed during China's recent Cultural Revolution and it is only lately that, aside from political posters, original art has emerged. The Yunnan School, for example, formed by Jiang Tie-Fang and fellow artists, expresses the belief that art is based on individual vision, not philosophy. The school established itself as a pioneer of contemporary art, but with the ideal of retaining a long view of Chinese art history. (Other modernists have joined together in movements known as Cynical Realism and Political Pop.)

As a note to history, during the 1980s/1990s over 40,000 tombs were looted: porcelain vases, statues, bronze vessels, and other antiquities were smuggled abroad and illegally sold.

Recently brought to the attention of the Western world is a royal treasure accumulated by Sung emperors of the 11th century down to early Chang emperors of the 18th century, consisting of paintings, scrolls, bronzes, jades, porcelains, jewelry, lacquerwork, and other decorative arts which had once numbered in the millions.

After departure of the last Manchu emperor from the Forbidden City in 1921, the Imperial Collection (built up through purchase, confiscation, gifts, and bribery) was seen shortly thereafter for the first time by the public. When an inventory was made, however, it was discovered that much of the collection had been looted.

When the Japanese invaded Manchuria, the art treasures, stored in approximately 20,000 boxes, began a journey that lasted 16 years. In 1945 the works were gathered together in Nanjing Museum, but when the communists began to take control, evacuation was made to Taiwan; the collection was placed in caves for 15 years. The Palace Museum in Taipei was established in 1965 when it was decided to create a permanent exhibition space. See Terra-Cotta Army and Thousand Buddha Caves.

Chinoiserie

The influence and adaptation of Chinese motifs and techniques in the Western world, especially in the decorative arts such as the Chinese style of porcelain making.

Chinoise Pop

A term descriptive of the work of Yung (1964-   ) whose Chinese Pop art depicts East meets West imagery: Eastern details of dress and style are commingled with Western themes. Classic is a diptych, titled *Easy Riders*, that portrays Asian motorcycle riders wearing costumes dating back to c. 500 B.C. See Neo-Iconography.

Cinquecento

Designating the 500s (1500s): an age of artistic genius. Leonardo da Vinci, Michelangelo, Raphael, Titian, Holbein, and many other great masters were active during this century. See High Renaissance.

"Circle of" or "Style of"

Followers of a certain artist who created art in a similar style such as the "Circle of Rubens" or the "Style of Poussin."

Cityscape

1. A view of a city or a part of it.
2. A term used to describe the ingredients of urban life such as street signs, skyscrapers, factories, and bridges.

Hill (1812-1879), as a topographical artist for the New York State Geological Survey, drew many views of American cities, which were published as lithographs; much admired was *New York From Brooklyn Heights*.

From 1905 to 1949 Sloan (1871-1951) created a large series of etchings devoted to New York City life.

When Kokoschka (1886-1980) toured European cities for seven years, his intention was to paint cosmic views of the cities that were expressive of his feelings. This series is called *The Painted World*.

Berthelsen (1883-1969), Marsh (1898-1954), and R. Soyer (1899-1987) are also known for their cityscapes of New York City. See Ash Can School, 14th Street School, and View Painting.

Classic

Referring to quality, not style. Monet's work would be regarded as classic or a typical example of Impressionism.

Classical Art

Referring to Greek, Roman, and Renaissance painting and sculpture. Simplicity, harmony, and balance are its underlying features. Most art forms recognized by the modern world can be traced to the classical world of art. Also, a term used to describe art of lasting quality.

Classical Revival

See Neoclassicism.

Classicism

1. Referring to return to the style and forms of art of the classical world. There have been two major periods of classicism in Western art, notably the years of the Renaissance and the period 1770-1830, designated as Neoclassicism.
2. Allegiance to traditional, universal standards.

Clip Art

Camera-ready art that is sold to newspapers and other publications which need small pieces of graphic art. Since there is no copyright, the purchaser can change the design. Clip art is available from low-cost books full of designs to high-quality work produced on single sheets.

Cloisonnism or the Pont-Aven Style

This style evolved from the paintings of Gauguin (1848-1903) and Bernard (1868-1941) who applied paint thinly and bound the unmodeled flat-colored areas with bold outlines; the effect of stained glass resulted. During this period, the artists were working out the theories of Synthetism, depending on the ideas of Symbolist poets. See Pont-Aven Group.

Closed Edition

See Limited Edition.

CoBrA (1948-1951)

A Dutch Expressionist movement led by Appel (1921-   ) and made up of experimental artists from Copenhagen, Brussels, and Amsterdam who wanted to explore the subconscious and fantastical imagery. Jorn (1914-1973) called it "an abstract art that does not believe in abstraction." It was a kind of surrealistic automatism fused with expressionistic figuration: unrestrained brushwork and wildly gestural forms resulted in visions from children's art, folk traditions, and primitivism. Many members are still active and its influence persists.

Codex (manuscript)

This term is meant to describe books containing separate leaves, in contrast to scrolls. Classic is a Late Roman or Early Christian book which served as a model for the production of religious texts. The practice was to preface the book with a portrayal of the author. The copyist then went on to decorate pages and to illustrate the narrative.

Codex Gates (recently called *Codex Hammer* or *Codex Leicester*)

A 72-page manuscript by Leonardo da Vinci, containing his musings on a wide-range field of scientific subjects, as well as 300 illustrations. Through the years, the manuscript has taken its current owner's name. (It is now owned by Bill Gates.)

Collage (mounting/pasting)

The technique of building up a picture in two-dimensional form or low relief, which emerged from the work of Picasso (1881-1973) and Braque (1882-1963). In essence, non-art materials (newspaper, wallpaper, and wood) were applied to the support with drawn or painted sketches made over the principal features of the subject. This technique is regarded as a turning point in 20th-century art: the language of Cubism was worked out through collage. See Papier Collé.

Collisionism (1990s)

As the theory of a new international movement, it has as its objective the creation of a new dynamism for the development of human society whereby new imagery can be transformed into kinetic energy. It is claimed this new basis for artistic thinking requires technical skill, ability to perceive the purity of artistic development, and professional knowledge from both the artist and the spectator.

Color Field Painting

A term that has been used to describe the work of many modernists who used color as both form and content. The artists created art suggestive of the sublime when they applied vast amounts of luminous color to huge canvases that produce lyrical or atmospheric effects. It was their intention that the paintings be viewed from a short distance to fill the mind with the object; the canvases, resembling total environments, seem to reach out to infinity, a kind of transcendental experience.

Rothko (1903-1970), Still (1904-1980), and Newman (1905-1970) are generally recognized as the pathfinders to this version of Abstract Expressionism. See Stain Painting and Zip Painting.

Colossus

An image or statue of very great size; it is a term that derives from statues of ancient times, especially those of Egypt and Mesopotamia. More recently are two American colossuses: *The Statue of Liberty* and *Freedom*. In modern times, a series of colossuses, titled *Hammering Man*, and measuring anywhere from 76 feet to lesser heights, have been designed by Borofsky (1942-   ); others include *Continuity* by Bill (1908-1995) and *Metrobot* by Paik (1932-   ).

Columbianum, The

The first American art academy, founded in 1794 by Chas. W. Peale; it was short-lived. See Museum and Peale Family.

Combine Painting

A term used to describe the assemblages of Rauschenberg (1925-   ), who uses bits of cultural flotsam and jetsam (postcards, magazine clippings, found objects, ready-mades), combined with canvas paintings, to show a fragmented view of reality. The artist said his combine paintings become "an adventure, like walking down the street."

Commercial Art

A craft involved with the aesthetic composition of words and images to convey commercial or social messages and ideas.

Commercial Artist

An artist commissioned to create work for a specific purpose such as advertisements or illustrations. See Illustrator and Poster.

Commodity Art

Objects and images are chosen from a commercial/industrial culture and presented in satirical settings as artworks: a kind of anti-sculpture.

Complex Forms

A group of generally unknown but related units.

Composed Objects

Objects are irrationally combined, as in Surrealism.

Composition

The arrangement of parts to present a unified artwork. Its components are order, balance, harmony, and clarity. Composition is a fundamental aspect of art because it communicates the vision of the artist and the meaning of his artwork to the viewer.

Computer Art or Cybernetic Art

The use of computers in the visual arts, allowing the imagination to soar in a way never before possible, began in the late 1960s. Several of its practical uses are:

1. As a sketch pad to make as many variations of an image as desired.
2. As a tool to manipulate and analyze the ideas and thoughts of the artist.
3. The writing of programs to construct modes of creative expression.
4. Mathematical calculations of shape and form.
5. Calculations of pigment proportions for color variations.
6. Images produced can be used in photographic reproduction.

See Cyberart, Cyberspace, and Information Art.

Computer Portrait Sculpture

A technique of sculpture initiated with a three-dimensional digitized image taken with a special lighting video camera and a computer set-up. A milling machine, controlled by the computer, then cuts the sculpture; this operation normally requires two or three hours for completion. The sculptor then sharpens some of the contours, after which the work is coated with epoxy and a bronze powder to make a proof. It is then sent to a foundry where a mold is made and the bronze is poured. By Cyberware Laboratories, California.

Conceptual Art (1960s-1970s)

A free-for-all range of activities whereby words or images communicate ideas. The artist intended that the viewer focus on the concept, rather than on the end product. LeWitt (1928-), one of its pioneers, said: "The idea becomes the machine that makes the art." Works are thus intended to appeal to the viewer's mind rather than to his eye.

The print media, as well as photography, film, and video, were the primary avenues of expression. Its underlying role was a great sense of liberation. See Art & Language, Fluxus, Happening, Performance Art, Process Art, and Word-Art.

Concrete Art (Konkrete Kunst)

A term used for nonfigurative art, without any reference to the object world: a synonym for nonobjective art as defined by Van Doesburg (1883-1931) in 1930.

Cone of Vision

The field of vision of the viewer of an artwork.

Confrontational Art

The preoccupation of Coe (1951-) with animal rights, urban problems, corruption, and the evils of war are depicted in drawings and paintings that provide scathing commentary on man's inhumanity to humankind and beast. See Revolutionary Art and Social Realism.

Connoisseurship

The love of anything is the fruit of our knowledge of it, and grows as our knowledge becomes more certain. (Leonardo da Vinci)

Conservator

A person responsible for the care, restoration, or repair of treasured artworks. During the process of restoration, the conservator must be able to combine a knowledge of painting materials and techniques with a deep understanding of the particular artist's approach to his work. Professional ethics demand that all alterations made to a painting must be reversible and the hand of the restorer remain invisible.

Constructions

Intangible qualities such as void, space, and depth are as important to sculptural forms as the tangible qualities of edge, volume, and mass. Objects are dissected so the space created within and around the form become integral parts of the composition. See Aerial Sculpture and Drawing in Space.

Construction-Sculpture

A large solid form is broken into smaller pieces. When it is assembled, with painted or sprayed colors applied, the construction captures the essence of having been drawn or painted in space. The materials used vary: found machine parts, steel or wood beams, and the like. See *Cubi Series* and Junk Art and Sculpture.

Constructivism (1914-1932)

A revolutionary movement concerned with a concept of sculpture, which was formulated by Malevich (1878-1935) and developed by the brothers Pevsner (1878-1962) and Gabo (1890-1977) in Moscow. Pevsner and Gabo published *Realistic Manifesto* in 1920; it proved to be a landmark in art history. The artists declared that space, movement, and time were essential elements of life; they rejected modeling, volume, and mass. (The relief sculptures of Tatlin (1885-1953) were also influential on the origins of Constructivism.)

Essentially, it was a functional art, often using factory-made materials, based on nonobjective, three-dimensional, sculptural forms with dynamic and spatial concepts. The artists held to the idea that their pure nonobjective forms would provide a model of harmony and stability in a chaotic world.

Constructivism opened the door to various techniques in the plastic arts, especially experimentation with light, space, and motion by a number of American artists. See Kinetic Sculpture and Mobile.

Russian Constructivist architecture had an extraordinary influence on modern European architecture, especially the Bauhaus and De Stijl.

Contemporary Art

It usually reflects the period in which the artist lives—according to the artist's perception or conception. It involves diverse styles, innovative techniques, and materials available.

Content

Although closely related, subject matter should not be confused with content. The latter is defined as the aesthetic, intellectual, spiritual, or narrative value of an artwork. Several paintings containing the same subject matter may express different values.

Form and content are the major elements of an artwork.

Continuous Style/Representation

1. An artistic technique which depicts several continuing episodes in one picture or relief sculpture — a form often used in Roman art. See Trajan's Column.
2. This was a common style in medieval fresco cycles and narrative paintings relating the lives of biblical figures.

Contour

The outline of a shape which is used to express movement, volume, or quality. It also refers to subtle modulation of light and dark tones.

Contrapposto (sometimes called weight-shift)

Referring to portrayal of the human body so that the upper portion moves in one direction and the lower portion in another, in an effort to create movement and tension. It was a device commonly used in classical Greek sculpture.

Conversation Pieces

These informal portraits, with subjects posed in groups of friends or family interacting and playing their roles in settings such as a garden or living room, can, perhaps, first be seen in the Western art world in the work of Anguissola (1532-1625) who painted pictures of her sisters in family groups.

This type of portraiture became popular in England during the 1700s. Classic is the work of Hogarth (1697-1764), who is known for satires on English family life. See Narrative Art.

Copy

A copy of a painting may have documentary or historical value. A gallery copy is executed by a professional copyist. A variant is a copy with changes made by the original artist or a copy made by an imitator. A replica is an exact copy done by the original artist or under his direction.

Corporate Art

A relatively new field in which corporations purchase contemporary art of known and unknown artists, most often with the assistance of art consultants. An important reason for the existence of Corporate art is it helps create an environment in which it is both enjoyable and profitable to do business. The underlying benefits, however, are that corporations are funding local, regional, and national arts organizations, as well as donating money and art to museums along with ideas and skills.

With political changes and a trend toward globalization, American and foreign companies are increasing their art sponsorship programs, either by sending exhibitions and projects to foreign countries, or by bringing programs from abroad to US institutions.

Cosmogenies

As a seminal figure of Nouveau Réalisme, Klein (1928-1962) experimented with the effect of rain on canvas covered with wet blue paint.

Court Painter

During centuries past, a master artist was invited by the nobility or the royalty to be the official court painter. The artist's main occupation was to paint or sculpt portraits of the household and others. Additional duties included the design of jewelry, furniture, weapons, and hall decorations. Anguissola, Collot, Holbein, Michelangelo, Rosse, Rubens, Ruysch, Velásquez, and Vigée-Lebrun are several master artists known to have worked as court painters, sometimes for short periods only and sometimes for years.

Craftsmanship

The use of tools and materials in a skillful manner. It includes sensitivity for and a knowledge and mastery of the materials used. In today's world, craftspersons are using high tech and advanced tools and materials to leverage the vision of the hand.

Crayon, The (1855-1861)

The first American magazine devoted to the arts. It was established in New York by John Durand, son of the artist Asher Durand, and by W. J. Stillman. While painting and architecture were its main subjects, topics also included sculpture, drama, poetry, music, and gardening.

Cryptogram

A drawing, painting, or writing with a hidden meaning.

Cubi Series

A series of machine-cut, stainless steel, abstract structures created by David Smith (1906-1965) from cubic forms of various dimensions that were arranged in solid geometric masses. They were intended to be seen outdoors as part of the landscape "colored by sky and surroundings." Smith's work was a major influence on contemporary sculpture. See Construction-Sculpture.

Cubism (1907-1925)

A term coined by the critic Vauxcelles. Contrary to common belief, however, the Cubist produces not only the cube, but also the polygon, the quadrilateral, the trapezoid, and the triangle.

Cézanne (1839-1906) is regarded as the forerunner of Cubism because of his structured style. The Cubist movement was initiated by Picasso (1881-1973) and Braque (1882-1963) who worked together in France to find new expression, a new way of seeing. Their discoveries began a new visual language (not a style) that relied on arrangements of planes and shapes rather than on color and perspective. It was adapted by many avant-garde artists according to their own interpretation of that language.

Its major approaches:

Analytical Cubism (breaking apart): The first stage (1907-1912) was a technique translated from collage into oil painting. Essentially, it was the presentation of different views of a subject in the same picture. The Cubist put into the picture what the mind knows exists—the other side of the figure or object — resulting in multiple viewpoints, with the parts being broken apart and then re-arranged, making it somewhat difficult to decipher, a sort of incomprehensible mental puzzle. Monochromatic, muted colors dominate. See Bateau-Lavoir Group.

Synthetic Cubism (building up or putting together): The composition began with the idea of a subject put together from both real and imaginary forms, a kind of drawing in space. One of the first attempts was when Picasso created a guitar from nonart materials and skillfully arranged them in three-dimensional space. Gris (1887-1927), regarded as a classic Syntheticist, worked primarily in the medium of collage; his primary aim was "to create new objects which cannot be compared with any object in reality." By the 1920s, Braque had developed another technique which he continued to practice until his death.

Rococo Cubism: A technique that Picasso and Braque created when both Analytical and Synthetic Cubism were combined in the same artworks.

Cubist Realism or Precisionism (1915-1920s)

The artists used the landscape of urban and industrial America: subjects, such as factories, ships, and bridges, were inspired by the machine age. Clean-edge forms were simplified to the point of abstraction: a kind of stylistic purity and strict simplicity of representation.

Bluemner (1867-1938)
Schamberg (1882-1918)
Demuth (1883-1935)
Sheeler (1883-1965)
O'Keeffe (1887-1986)

Cubist Sculpture

Cubism was initially a way of breaking down and re-arranging form. Nonetheless, its simplifications could be and were applied to sculpture: during the Synthetic stage of Cubism, sculptors adapted its principles to their creations. It probably signified the most dramatic change in the techniques and forms of sculpture since antiquity: Cubist sculptures were not just solid figures with faceted planes, but also involved interpenetration of space.

Duchamp-Villon (1876-1918)
González (1876-1942)
Laurens (1885-1954)
Archipenko (1887-1964)
Lipchitz (1891-1973)

See Aerial Sculpture.

Cubo-Futurism (1913-1915)

Rather than an art movement, it was more a theory expounded by the Russian poet Kruchenykh who said: "Art goes in the vanguard of psychic evolution." It represented art of the transcendent, something outside ordinary human experience, in the hope the consciousness would be altered to a state similar to that achieved by Yoga discipline. Its adherents believed everything in the universe had an inner being, that nothing was inanimate. See Rayonism, Suprematism, and Zaum.

Curator

The functions of a curator are complex. Aside from being a scholar and a connoisseur, he/she must serve the public and advise and convince trustees on the importance of new acquisitions. In today's world, the curator's main duties are:

1. The care of artworks.
2. The exhibition of artworks best suited to produce their aesthetic and educational importance.

Currier & Ives (1857-1907)

A printmaker who mass-produced prints ("Coloured Engravings for the People") depicting contemporary American life. The most common subjects: landscape views, historic events, allegorical scenes, portraiture, and sports. In all, about 7,000 scenes were reproduced. One of the best known is *Home for Thanksgiving* by Durrie (1820-1862). Although many renderings of events or genre scenes are highly exaggerated or idealized, Currier & Ives prints provide a guide to American culture and taste of the 1800s and constitute an integral part of American art.

Cyberart

Digital art available on-line or in CD-ROM, created specifically for the medium, often allowing for interaction.

Cyberdesign

Referring to ways in which to explore the world in future years: reality and the hypothetical are explored for the possibility of new technology. Ideas and research result in conceptual prototypes.

Cyberspace

The environment in and through which all computer interactivity takes place. Classic is a Performance art of interactive, computer-generated pictures and words made possible by NAPLPS (North American Presentation Level Protocol Syntax), a code that wraps pictures and words together.

Native American artists in particular have applied this technique; it has enabled them to create bold graphics in sequence that can be transmitted to any computer screen. Their "art gallery" exists only in cyberspace: mechanics, human imagination, and computerized telecommunications are used to tell stories and to make cross-cultural exchanges.

Cycle Series

Paintings linked by theme. Classic are the fresco cycles in churches and public buildings in Italy of the 14th/15th centuries, containing religious and humanistic themes.

In more recent times, classic is a cycle of 11 allegorical works rendered by de Callatäy (1932-), titled *Symphony for Christine*, that are arranged in four movements: scenes symbolizing desire, caring, love, and death.

D

Dada (1916-1922)

An international movement that grew out of WWI, formed by artists, poets, and writers. It radically altered the course of artistic creation in this century. Basically, the participants were against the past and the future, affirming that nothing more was to be said. They ridiculed human activities and feelings in artworks that form a mosaic of styles and, generally, tried to create as big a scandal as possible in the exploration of new techniques of expression such as nonsensical poetry and disorganized events and performances. The mediums of collage, typography, photography, cinema, constructions, paintings, and posters were used as tools to represent nothing at all. It was a kind of black humor. Grosz (1893-1959) stated it was "the organized use of insanity to express contempt for a bankrupt world."

Despite the negative outlook of Dada, it helped artists to discover and make use of chance effects for artistic creation. See Fluxus, Photomontage, and Surrealism.

Danube School (1500s)

Referring to those artists active in Austria and Bavaria, who used lush landscape and rich color as a vital part of their representations of the moods of nature.

Day Without Art and Night Without Light

An international event that commemorates people in the art world who have died of AIDS.

Deaccession

The selling of treasured objects or artworks by a museum. Because of strict standards, this practice is only tolerated by the American Association of Museum Directors if proceeds received from sales are used to purchase more art—not to pay for operating costs of the museum. Their philosophy is that museums exist to protect their collections, not the reverse.

Death Mask

A plaster cast molded onto the face of the deceased—a practice popular during Roman times—to commemorate ancestors. See Faiyum Portrait.

Deattribution

An artwork that is no longer recognized as having been rendered by a named artist is deattributed.

Décalcomania

A technique developed by Surrealist artists, most notably Dominguez (1901-1956) who placed a newly painted surface against a second surface. In the process, a spontaneous blurred effect was created. The images of animals, wheels, and rocks are regarded as his best works. Ernst (1891-1976) pressed two newly painted canvases together and then pulled them apart. He used the resulting patterns as starting points for new paintings. See Frottage.

Décollage: Les Affichistes (poster designers)

A technique of Nouveau Réalisme in which a torn or disfigured poster is proof that the hypnotic power of advertising is destroyed. Rotella (1918-   ) is believed to have been the pioneer of this process. He said it was "the only way of protesting against a society that has lost the taste for transformation. . . ."

Deconstruction

Referring basically to architects who challenge conventional thought about the nature of building design. In general, artists and architects inspired by this challenge want to create works that confound traditional expectations. See Videopavilion.

Decorative Art

1. An artwork that fits and harmonizes with a plan of interior design.
2. The decoration of interiors with trompe l'oeil scenes or designs: furniture, walls, floors, and ceilings are the usual supports.

Decorative Arts (sometimes called Applied Art or the Minor Arts)

Aesthetic, historical, and cultural origins are translated into decorative objects that reflect motifs of contemporary society. Classic are the high-quality productions of such historic names as Gallé, Tiffany, and Weller. See Art Nouveau and Art Deco.

Decorative-Arts Images

During the 19th century, manufacturers of all sorts of household goods, including cabinet makers, porcelain makers, and upholsterers, produced carefully rendered engravings of their wares, showing a wealth of detail. While some images showed a single piece of furniture, other engravings showed fully decorated room settings. Many of the original watercolor studies have survived intact. See Print.

Decoupage

The application of cutouts to a surface. This process is used in creating collages. See Papier Découpé.

Degenerate Art (Entartete Kunst) (1933-1937)

A term applied to the exhibition of Modern art in Germany by the Nazis, who confiscated and exhibited artworks in an attempt to discredit modern artists. In reality, many of the artworks were auctioned off for the financial benefit of the Nazis; other works were either lost or intentionally destroyed. The artists themselves were either banned, exiled, or imprisoned because Hitler was determined to wage a relentless war of purification against Modern art. It is estimated more than 16,000 artworks were expropriated during this period, including those taken from museums.

Official art of the Nazi regime was called "Neo-Classical." Generally, it consisted of mythological subjects idealizing Germans as heroic descendants of ancient Greeks, along with paintings of conventional landscapes, animal scenes, still lifes, glorifications of motherhood, and portraiture of high Nazi officials. See Kunstschutz.

Derivative

Referring to subject matter appropriated or borrowed from the work of other artists. See Appropriated.

Desacralization

The travesty of sacred-like art subjects such as the *Mona Lisa* with a beard and mustache.

Design

An arrangement of colors, lines, forms, or patterns. Its components are unity/ variety, scale/proportion, balance, rhythm, and emphasis.

De Stijl

Look under S.

Detail

A small or minute part of an artwork. When reproduced in a book or magazine, it is enlarged to provide a close-up view of texture and color.

Detonography

A technique practiced by E. Rosenberg (1942-) who molds plaster onto a panel, occasionally adding found objects or impressions. Thereafter, the mold is taken to a blasting range where it is covered with a sheet of metal and plastic explosive. After explosion, a perfect replica of the mold has been transferred to the metal sheet. The result is a bas-relief executed in fine detail.

Deutscher Werkbund (1907-1933)

A progressive German association of manufacturers, architects, artists, and designers, formed by the architect Muthesius (1861-1927) to promote quality in the disciplines of art and architecture. It had a widespread influence on other European countries.

DIAS (Destruction in Art Symposium) (1960s)

A Dada-like movement active in England and the US, which was formed to participate in activities such as "Destruction Happenings" and "Destruction Events." See Fluxus.

Digital-Imaging

Rather than using regular sketching tools, the artist renders drawings with electronic styluses and computerized tablets.

The Dinner Party inspired by Chicago (1939-   )

A triangular table, 48 feet in length per side, with 39 place settings, celebrating women in history and in legend and testifying to their artistic and cultural contributions: an icon of Feminist art. The piece incorporates sculpture, weaving, china painting, and needlework. Hundreds of women worked on it. Other long-term mixed media pieces are *The Birth Project* and *The Holocaust Project.*

Diorama (usually miniature in size)

1. A scenic representation in which a painting is seen through an opening.
2. A scenic representation with sculpted figures, realistic detail, and a painted background. See Presepio.

Diptych

1. A painting or altarpiece consisting of two parts.
2. An artwork made of two matching parts.

Distemper

A technique of painting, as distinguished from tempera, in which powdered colors are mixed with size, gum, or whitening and dispersed in water. Its principal use is for scene-painting.

Distortion

A lack of proportionality. In Modern art, a deviation from convention in the rendition of color, form, or perspective.

"Disturbatory" Art

A term coined by the philosopher A. Danto to describe artworks that depict Realism in extremis: blood, pain, excrement, mutilation, obscenity, and death—in contrast to the work of artists commenting on the problems and situations of everyday life, as in Social Realism.

Another vogue term is "Abject" art, coined by J. Kristeva, to designate art based on the image of the human body: a body fragmented or decayed or possibly represented in a socially unacceptable function. The theory is that art breaks through societal taboos.

Divisionism

See Neo-Impressionism.

Docent

A person who is an extension of the education department of a museum and conducts guided tours.

Documenta

An exhibition that takes place every four or five years in Kassel, Germany. The first one, in 1955, had as its purpose the renewal of German culture after the Nazi era.

In later years, it celebrated the importance of modern movements such as Minimalism, Pop art, and Video art. More recently, it has advertised itself "as the largest and most expansive contemporary art show ever mounted."

Donor Portraiture

During the Middle Ages, many paintings or altarpieces contained the portrayal of a seemingly devout spectator who was, in reality, the donor of the artwork. The artwork was usually commissioned as an offering of gratitude or devotion or in fulfillment of a vow. (Occasionally, members of the donor's family were also portrayed.) Classic is *The Madonna of Chancellor Rolin* by Jan van Eyck (1385-1441). See Ex-Voto.

Double-Image

A drawing or painting that is rendered so the viewer perceives two separate images: a tree may resemble a foot or a hand.

Drawing

As an essential part of artistic activity, its techniques are varied. Three major approaches:

1. Delineative drawing (all lines).
2. Form drawing (light and shadow effects).
3. Color value drawing (tonal value, as in painting).

Its various mediums include chalk, charcoal, crayon, ink, metal point, and pencil. Sketching is done spontaneously in a short period of time, representing a more casual approach, in contrast to the studied approach of a subject used in drawing. Ingres' dictum: "Drawing is the integrity of art."

Drawing in Space

A term describing the sculptural work of Lassaw (1913-) who bent, welded, and soldered wire into strong, organic form. His first abstract work in 1931 made him a pioneer of abstract sculpture in the US.

Hunt (1935-), known for large public sculptures, notably *Jacob's Ladder*, often refers to his wall pieces as "drawings in space." He said: "Sometimes I try to develop forms nature might create if only heat and steel were available to her."

Drip Painting

The technique of applying paint by dripping, splattering, or pouring onto canvas. The artists known for this technique include Hofmann (1880-1966), Pollock (1912-1956), and Francis (1923-1994). See Action Painting.

Droit de Suite (artists' proceeds rights)

In recent years, there has been international controversy as to whether or not artists (or their heirs) are entitled to a percentage of a sales price every time an artwork is sold for profit. In the US, to date, California seems to be the only state that has mandated payment of a percentage of any sales price (over $1,000) to be paid to the artist or to his/her heirs by the dealer or seller. (The law allows payment to an estate within 20 years of an artist's death.)

Droit Moral (moral right)

According to French law, artists' widows/widowers and other family members have the inherited right to be the legal authenticators of their relatives' work.

Duco Paint

The use of automobile enamel by some modern-day artists.

Dummy-Board Figures

Life-size cutouts of human figures, painted in oils, are placed in genre and domestic scenes. They were popular in the 1800s when they were used as fire screens or for decorative purposes. Currently, dummy-board figures seem to be making a small comeback.

Dutch School

A. Bloemaert (1564-1651)
Hals (1580-1666)
van Honthorst (1590-1656)
Claesz (1594-1680)
van Campen (1595-1657)
van Goyen (1596-1656)
Jansz (1597-1665)
H. Bloemaert (1601-1672)
Rembrandt (1606-1669)
Dou (1613-1675)
Both (1615-1652)
Ter Borch (1617-1681)
de Witte (1617-1692)
Kalf (1619-1693)
van Bayeren (1620-1690)
Cuyp (1620-1691)
Fabritius (1622-1654)
Steen (1626-1679)
van Aelst (1626-1683)
van Ruisdael (1628-1682)
Metsu (1629-1667)
de Hooch (1629-1677)
Vermeer (1632-1675)
van der Heyden (1637-1712)
Hobbema (1638-1709)
van de Velde (1642-1679)
van de Cappelle (1642-1679)

E

Early American Art

Although the first settlers brought with them a rich European culture, in their struggles they held to the idea that the arts were largely for practical purposes. According to newspaper ads, "painting in general" included the decoration of carriages, floors, and furniture, the creation of trade signs and painted tinware, house decorations, and portraiture. These productions contributed to the formation of the first regional style in the Colonies. See Folk Art.

In the fine arts, painters were usually limited to portraiture. See Limners. The first school of American painting developed in the Hudson River Valley. See Patroon Painters.

During the 1700s, the crafts of the furniture maker, the goldsmith, and the silversmith flourished; they were regarded as prestigious professions.

The first art exhibition is believed to have been held by Smibert (1688-1751) when he opened his studio in 1730 to show his collection of paintings after Old Masters and portraits of leading citizens of Boston. See Museum.

Five Early American painters, namely, Copley, West, Peale, Stuart, and Trumbull, have been referred to as the touchstone of American art. In various ways, these artists were responsible for the birth of painting in America. See American School and Peale Family.

Early Christian Art

The Early Christians buried the dead in catacombs that were painted in earthen colors and decorated with illusionistic representations. These are the best-known paintings. During the age of persecution, artists used a code of symbols. There was little wealth among the Early Christians, which resulted in the creation of a simple but fine art in the form of wall frescoes. In later years, art took the form of narrative relief to illustrate biblical themes. See Byzantine Art and Sarcophagus.

Early Renaissance (the 1400s: Quattrocento)

Florence, as the new Athens, was hailed as the champion of freedom as well as the home of arts and crafts. As such, it offered opportunities for diverse creative talents. Painting was reclassified as a liberal art. In this new place of high esteem, the artist was looked upon as a person of learning and culture.

Donatello (1386-1466), a sculptor, and Brunelleschi (1377-1446), an architect, as well as Alberti (1404-1472), an architect and writer who established the principles of naturalism through perspective and the dramatic composition of figures, are regarded as founding fathers of the Renaissance.

Artful perspective, chiaroscuro, and the realistic rendering of face and form became characteristic of Italianate painting. Uccello (1397-1475) and Masaccio (1401-1428) were among the first painters to master the illusion of three dimensionality. See High Renaissance.

Earth Art, Land Art, or Earthworks (1960s-1990s)

A view of natural inland scenery involving the re-arrangement, shifting, and cutting of portions of the earth, enabling the spectator to see the land as a presence with abstract suggestions. Some of the works, however, have been destructive.

Earth art also indicates an interest in ecology and nostalgia for past ages: ruins, geology, and prehistory; in painting, it appears in poetic nature-images.

Herd (1950-) renders American Indian designs, portraits, and advertisements in large fields of vacant land. His "brushes" are hoes and weed clippers. The work is best seen from an airplane. See Transitory Artworks.

Easel Painting

A movable framed painting to be displayed on an easel. See Cabinet Painting.

Eccentric Abstraction

A term coined by the critic Lippard to describe the adjoining of Minimalism and Surrealism. Classic is the work of Hesse (1936-1970) who used materials, such as papier-mâché, rope, string dipped in fiberglass, and cheesecloth, to create boxes, webs, and planes. See Post-Minimalism.

Eclecticism

The practice of appropriating and combining the best features from various styles and techniques in the hope of producing a new style: the absence of a personal style by the artist.

Edinburgh International Festival

Since 1947, this city has been the site for multi-cultural festivals lasting three weeks: performing, visual, musical, and celluloid works are celebrated in a mix of events.

Eggbeater Series

Davis (1894-1964) mastered Cubism by doing variations of one still life for a year: a series of abstract paintings in which he attempted to rid himself of any illusion by repeatedly painting an eggbeater, an electric fan, and a rubber glove until they ceased to exist except as color, line, and shape. See Modern Art.

Egyptian Art (3200-332 B.C.)

Egyptian art was uncommonly self-contained; it remained constant for more than 30 centuries, content with its own conventions. Artists had to learn and comply with a set of strict rules.

Its art forms were usually related to architecture (pyramids, temples, obelisks) and sculpture. Paintings on walls, on pottery, and on other useful objects were marked by strong line, regular pattern, harmony, flatness, lack of emotion, descriptive perspective, and a multitude of colors.

Egyptian artists were the first to explore the world of human relationships, especially celebrating the dignity of family life.

Aristocratic Egyptians were concerned with the happy afterlife and preservation of the body. They saw art as the keynote in service to the gods. Tombs were heavily decorated with painted reliefs narrating the lives of decedents; statues were placed at the doors of tombs and within enlarged temple districts.

Monumental sculpture in large stone statues represented gods, kings, and the nobility. In colossal form, on occasion, statues fused with architecture. As the years passed, metalwork and sculpture became quite advanced. Egyptian achievements were influential on Greek and Roman art.

The Eight (1904-1908)

A group of highly individual artists who exhibited together in New York City and nine other American cities in 1908. They shared a belief in the power of independent exhibitions, the recording of everyday life as vital subject matter for fine art, and the honest portrayal of their own experiences, attitudes, and beliefs. In sum, each artist combined in his paintings, drawings, and prints an individual view of American life and the European modernist aesthetic.

With this exhibition, the artists assumed a leading position in contemporary art: they were perceived to be the most progressive artists in the US when they defied Victorian niceties of traditional artists with images that exposed the realities of urban life. In addition, their work constituted an important milestone in the development of American Realism. (Several members were referred to as the Ash Can School.)

Prendergast (1859-1924)
Davies (1862-1928)
Henri (1865-1929)
Luks (1867-1933)
Glackens (1870-1938)
Sloan (1871-1951)
Lawson (1873-1939)
Shinn (1876-1953)
Bellows (1882-1925)

See American Realism, American Scene Painting, Armory Show, and Cityscape.

El Paso (1957-1960)

A group of artists who wanted to establish Spain as a creative center and to encourage other painters of Expressive Abstraction. Their revolutionary object was "the free unfolding of art and the artist." See Art Informel.

Encaustic Painting

Colors are mixed with molten beeswax and resin before application to the painting surface. It was one of the principal techniques of painting in Egypt, Greece, and Rome. Its exact formula has been lost.

Engaged

A sculpture that is not free standing; rather, it is attached to another element.

English School

Hilliard (1547-1619)
Mutens (1590-1642)
van Dyck (1599-1641)
Cooper (1609-1672)
Riley (1646-1691)
Dahl (1656-1743)
Hogarth (1697-1764)
Hayman (1708-1776)
Ramsay (1713-1784)
Wilson (1714-1782)
Reynolds (1723-1792)
Stubbs (1724-1806)
Sandby (1725-1809)
Gainsborough (1727-1788)
Barrett (1732-1784)
Romney (1734-1802)
Towne (1739-1816)
Cozens (1752-1799)
Raeburn (1756-1823)
Crome (1768-1821)
Lawrence (1769-1830)
Girtin (1775-1802)
Turner (1775-1851)
Constable (1776-1837)
Callcott (1799-1844)
Cotman (1782-1842)
Cox (1783-1859)
Frith (1819-1909)

Environmental Art or Eco Art

Art is now being used as a tool to raise the public consciousness for the environment and for protection of animals. Poster art is a common medium. See Art of Denunciation.

Environmental Sculpture

Classic are the enormous concrete, brick, and steel constructions of Holt (1938-), usually sited in deserts or urban park settings where emphasis is placed on space and relativity of scale. One of her most well-known works is *Dark Star Park* in Rosslyn, Virginia; it occupies two-thirds of an acre. See Space Exploration.

Environments/Assemblages (1950s-1960s)

The combination of the qualities of painting, sculpture, collage, theatre, and spectator participation. See Sculpto-Pictoramas.

Ephemera Collecting

Referring to the collection of disposable items, usually from years past: a sort of discovery of everyday life of another age, a paper archeology evoking other eras, other times, other spaces. Vintage postcards, old movie posters, baseball cards, and graphics of household products, all created in rich, vibrant color, are regarded as art by serious collectors.

Equestrian Portrait/Sculpture

A portrait or statue usually of a great personage seated on a horse. Classic is *Charles V on Horseback* by Titian (1490-1576), the first painting of its kind. Although the scene is artificial, it created a powerful image that remained influential for decades.

Ethnographic Art

The art inspired by a racial culture and especially referring to Primitive art.

Etruscan Art (600s-400s B.C.)

Before Roman growth, the Etruscans were a confederation of city-states in Italy. Their artistic expression was reflected in large and small bronze or painted terra-cotta sculptures, portrait busts, and vase painting. Mural work and painted reliefs located in elaborate tombs depicted scenes from daily life; other times the funeral feast was shown. Architecture and town planning were extraordinary. Minor arts were ivory carving and metalwork: they were exceptional metalsmiths.

When the Romans displaced the Etruscans, the Greek background of Etruscan art carried over.

Eucalyptus School (1915-1930)

A title used to cover numerous landscape artists once active in Southern California. Their decorative paintings, executed with loose brushwork and bland, pastel coloration, depict scenes of local areas.

Euston Road Group (1930s)

Referring to English painters who turned to simplicity and a naturalistic style in the rendition of genre, landscapes, portraits, and still lifes.

Expressionism

Referring to both a style in art and a 20th-century movement. Throughout the history of art, artists have used exaggeration, distortion of form, color, or space to express inner feelings.

The term "Expressionism," however, was adopted in the early 1900s to describe revolutionary art movements that arose in Germany when artists began to paint with strong color, distorted form, and bold, loose brushwork. Figural imagery was a vital element and color was used as an independent force because the artists thought of it as symbolic or as creating movement.

Although Matisse and the Fauve painters are credited with its innovation in modern times, it was essentially a German movement. El Greco (1541-1614) might be called the first Expressionist, but in Modern art van Gogh (1853-1890) can be referred to as the father of Expressionism because of his style and his subjective feelings about the painted object. The Norwegian artist Munch (1863-1944) was its most dominant influence in Northern Europe. See German Expressionism.

Expressionist Realism (1914-1930s)

An important style in France: artists expressed a natural spontaneity in the rendition of still lifes, nude portraiture, and landscapes.

Ex-Voto

1. An artwork designated to give thanks for a miraculous favor or in fulfillment of a vow.
2. A religious painting donated as an offering to a saint in time of trouble and often including written descriptions and requests. See Retablo and Santos.

F

Fabricated Art

An art form regarded as revolutionary: an art of idea and not of object. The artist licenses or sells the unrealized work — a working drawing; the purchaser has the right to construct it according to instructions from the artist.

Factura (early 1900s)

Cubism, as developed in Russia, in which multiple planes and the breaking up of objects were the techniques in creating collages. It was a strong influence on Constructivism.

Faiyum Portrait

A type of funerary portrait found in Egypt from about the 1st century to the 4th century A.D. It was painted in tempera or encaustic, enclosed in a wrapping, and placed close to the face of the deceased person.

Far Distance or Offskip

A scene or representation which appears farthest from the eye of the viewer.

Fauve Painting (1904-1908)

The artists were called "les Fauves" (wild beasts) by the critic Vauxcelles after viewing their work. Although the artists had formulated no doctrine, their work was characterized by thick line, energy, and distortion. Pure (straight from the tube), brilliant, explosive and, at times, wildly unrealistic, hallucinatory color was applied with small, crude brushstrokes to canvases filled with simplified, primitive imagery. The major theme was the landscape of tourist meccas: villages, cities, countrysides, seaside resorts, and the coastline. Their secondary theme was the activities of people.

Matisse (1869-1954), their informal leader, said: "Fauve painting isn't everything, only the beginning of everything."

Roualt (1871-1958)
Levy (1875-1944)
Marquet (1875-1947)
Vlaminck (1876-1958)
Puy (1876-1960)
van Dongen (1877-1968)
Derain (1880-1954)
Braque (1882-1963)
Thompson-Zorach (1887-1968)

See Expressionism.

Federal Art Project (1933-1943)

This project was created during the Great Depression for the purpose of employing artists, educating art students, expanding art programs in rural areas, and recording the cultural heritage of the US. More that 2 million students of all races attended classes in New York alone.

The statistics show that artists produced approximately 100,000 paintings, 18,000 sculptures, 2,500 murals, and thousands of posters, prints, photographs, and other works. Much of the work was for the adornment of public buildings such as schools, hospitals, and government buildings.

Thousands of these artworks, however, were either destroyed, auctioned off in bales as "used canvas," or wrapped around ducts for insulation. Nevertheless, the project was regarded as a great success. Many of the artists who worked for this project are well known today. See WPA.

"Feminine" Art

Traditionally, during centuries past, miniatures, pastels, portraits, still lifes, illuminated manuscripts, and crafts.

Feminist Art

The theme of artist/woman is found in the work of many women who recognize their own lives as proper subject matter. Kahlo (1907-1954) has been called la patrona (the patron saint) of Feminist art; Chicago (1939-   ) is regarded as another strong exponent.

Femmage

A term coined by Schapiro (1923-   ) to describe her colorful work in which elements of collage consisting of pieces of feminine fabric (lace, chintz, and gingham) are combined with Abstract art.

Fêtes Galantes (feasts of courting)

A term coined by the French Academy in 1717. It applies to any open-air scene with a mixed company, all enjoying themselves outdoors. Classic are the scenes set in idyllic park-like surroundings, with figurative subjects acting in a graceful or frivolous manner. Watteau (1684-1721) was the innovator of this theme; in part, it constitutes the essence of French 18th-century painting. See Rococo.

Fiber Art

Several of its techniques are weaving, macramé, needlework, and quilting; its history can be traced to millenniums past as a tribal craft. One innovator of this art form, Zeisler (1903-1991), created free-form fiber sculptures. The artist regarded the special process used by her in the creation of complex woven works as a personal trademark.

Field

The flat space or plane, defined by its edges, within which the artist works.

Figural Archaism

A term coined by the critic D. Kuspit to describe the ceramic and bronze sculptures of DeStaebler (1933-   ), which resemble historical artifacts. His fragmented, dismembered forms seem to evoke reference to religious art and classical sculpture.

Figurative Art

The depiction of recognizable shapes or images, which need not be realistic. See Representational Art.

Figurative Expressionism

Several generations of the New York School turned to the figure as their motif. Their approaches to this style, however, widely differ.

Figureheads

From earliest times, figures of either humans or animals have been placed at the prows of sailing vessels. In the US, the symbolic polychromed carvings on ships have long been prized as an important Folk art. Ship carvers, most notably the Skillin family in the 18th/19th centuries, made figureheads and other work for virtually every ship of importance. "The grand period of American marine decoration" was inaugurated by Rush (1756-1833), who carved figures full of motion and dynamic concepts, rather than the stiff figures of prior years.

Fine Arts

Essentially, those arts which can be enjoyed for their own sake: painting, drawing, sculpture, and the graphic arts. The term "fine arts" was not used until the 1400s because prior to that time painters, artisans, and craftspersons were in the same category. See Renaissance.

Fine Paintings

A term used to describe the paintings produced during the Golden Age of Dutch Painting. The artists reproduced nature as though reflected in a mirror: technical virtuosity and narrative skills were outstanding.

Finish Fetishists

A Southern California school of painters who favor the lustrous finishes created by industrial processes. The artists use metallic paints and the technologies of plastics fabrication to conceal the hand of the artist.

Flemish School

Master of Flémalle (1378-1444)
Limbourg Brothers
(active 1399-1439)
Hubert van Eyck (d. 1426)
Jan van Eyck (1385-1441)
van der Weyden (1400-1464)
Christus (1410-1472)
Bouts (1415-1475)
Memling (1430-1494)
van der Goes (1444-1482)
Bosch (1450-1516)
David (1450-1523)
A. Bening (d. 1519)
Massys (1466-1530)
Grossaert (1478-1533)
S. Bening (1483-1561)
Patinir (1485-1525)
van Sorel (1495-1562)
Brueghel (1525-1569)
Rubens (1577-1640)

Florentine School

Cimabue (1240-1302)
Cavallini (1250-1330)
Giotto (1266-1336)
Bicci (1373-1452)
Fra Angelico (1387-1455)
del Castagno (1390-1457)
Uccello (1397-1475)
DiGiusto (1400-1450)
Venziano (1400-1451)
Masaccio (1401-1428)
Fra Lippi (1406-1469)
Pollaiuolo (1429-1498)
Messina (1430-1479)
Verrocchio (1435-1488)
Signorelli (1441-1523)
Botticelli (1444-1510)
Dom. Ghirlandaio (1449-1494)
Leonardo da Vinci (1452-1519)
Dav. Ghirlandaio (1452-1525)
Fil. Lippi (1457-1504)
B. Ghirlandaio (1458-1497)
Di Credi (1458-1537)
DiCosimo (1462-1521)
Fra Bartolommeo (1475-1517)
Michelangelo (1475-1564)
del Sarto (1486-1531)

Fluxus (1962-1978)

A Dada-like, ephemeral, loose collective of like-minded spirits formed by an international group of young artists, poets, writers, film makers, and composers. Because it was anti-authoritarian and quarrelsome, it had no base except that under the guidance of G. Maciunas, a graphic designer, Soho in Manhattan was established as an art community. He described Fluxus as a "fusion of Spike Jones, vaudeville gag, children's games and Duchamp." Fluxus artists believed that everyday actions, gestures, and language should be regarded as art.

Central to its theme: irreverence, inversion, surprise, and irrationality. In its various formats (new music, performances, multimedia installations, mail art, experimental films, street events, games, surreal objects, artists' books, posters, and newsletters), Fluxus encompassed the most dramatic events of the era; it helped give birth to major art forms such as Conceptual, Performance, and Video art.

In 1992, the 30th anniversary of Fluxus was celebrated in both Europe and the US in exhibitions called "Flux Attitudes," "In the Spirit of Fluxus," and "10 Years on Broadway: Fluxus, 1982-1992." Works are documented in *Fluxus Code* by J. Hendricks.

Currently, younger artists are again pushing at the borders between art and reality, asserting that everyday objects, materials, and events constitute art.

Folk Art or Peasant Art

It has been known, fundamentally, as a simple art created by a rural, nonindustrial people: objects used every day such as weather vanes, toys, trade signs, wood carvings, furniture, pottery, boxes, hooked rugs, samplers, and quilts. Changing fashions or tastes are not reflected because traditional patterns and designs continue through the decades. Timeless themes such as religion, cultural heritage, and patriotism are important sources of inspiration and imagery. (In American Folk art, the written word is strongly identified with religious works of the 1900s, particularly in the South.)

Generally, three areas dominate:

1. Decorative crafts pertaining to a distinct cultural group.
2. Anonymous paintings and sculptures produced for practical reasons.
3. Paintings and sculptures by naive or self-taught artists.

Today, much handcraftsmanship has been rendered unnecessary as mass-produced products and new technologies have been developed. See Calligraphy Drawings, Carousel Figures, Figureheads, Fraktur, Macramé, Mass Art, Memory Paintings, Mourning Pictures, Naive Art, Santos, Show Figures, Theorem Painting, Tramp Art, and Whirligig.

Forces Nouvelles (1930s)

An association of painters in Paris whose ambition was to create a new, expressive naturalism relating to modern life.

Foreground

A scene or representation which appears closest to the viewer or in the lower portion of the painting, especially in landscapes, cityscapes, and seascapes.

Form

1. A three-sided effect created through structural drawing or perspective.
2. The arrangement of parts of an artwork.
3. Referring to fullness, solidity, and structure: an artistic reality.
4. Descriptive terms, such as basic, complex, expressive, free, functional, geometric, etc., may be applied.

Nature produces the material, but genius brings forth the form. (Alberti)

Formalism

A term coined by the critic C. Greenberg to designate his theory that art of the 20th century is a search for pure, abstract form: a systematic removal of subject matter or subjective feelings, as in Color Field Painting, or painting that defines itself by its own purely visual properties of flatness, shape, and color.

Found Object (objet trouvé)

1. Natural objects, such as driftwood or seashells which are found by chance, become part of three-dimensional artworks.
2. A fragment of a man-made object chosen for its inner beauty or aesthetic value.

Dienes (1898-1992) used sundry materials: "the squishes and squashes on the street . . . nothing is so humble that it cannot be made into art" was her artistic credo.

Four, Los

A group of Chicano artists who had numerous exhibitions in the 1970s. They have achieved recognition on both a regional and national level. See Hispanic Art in the US.

14th Street School (1920s-1930s)

Caught up in the color, humanity, and fabric of New York City life, this group of artists living in the vicinity of 14th Street painted their immediate environment—the city itself and ordinary, everyday people doing ordinary, everyday things. The artists wanted to create a meaningful urban art; they are regarded as the second generation of the Ash Can School.

Fragmentation

In artistic usage, it is a deliberate disassembling and re-arranging.

Fraktur

Referring to an American Folk art in the form of an illuminated manuscript. It was brought to the New World by immigrants from Northern Europe who settled in Pennsylvania in the late 1600s. Birth and baptismal certificates, family records, and valentines were some of the items produced using this technique.

Free Form

Not restricted to conventional form: any curvilinear, asymmetrical shape not bound by hard edges.

Free Standing

Standing alone or on its own foundation without a background.

French School

Clouet (1486-1540)
Cousin (1490-1560)
DeLyon (1500-1574)
A. LeNain (1588-1648)
L. LeNain (1593-1648)
G. La Tour (1593-1652)
Vignon (1593-1670)
Poussin (1594-1665)
Claude Lorrain (1600-1682)
M. LeNain (1607-1677)
Largilliere (1654-1746)
Watteau (1684-1721)
Chardin (1699-1779)
Fragonard (1732-1806)
David (1748-1825)
Lebrun (1755-1842)
Michel (1763-1843)
Ingres (1780-1867)
Corot (1796-1875)
Delacroix (1798-1863)
Daumier (1808-1879)
T. Rousseau (1812-1867)
Courbet (1819-1877)

See Paris, School of

Fresco

An ancient technique for the painting of walls or ceilings to make a lasting picture. Pigments are crushed in water and applied to wet plaster on the wall. This art form calls for precision, rapidity of execution, and supreme confidence. (Fresco secco refers to the technique of applying paint to dry plaster.)

The medium of fresco reached full height during the 1300s/1400s in Italy when walls and ceilings of churches, palaces, and public buildings were covered with vast murals. (Giotto of the Florentine School was the first great master of fresco.)

As a note to history, during the 1300s frescoes were regarded as "poor people's art." The scenes painted were intended to teach Christians about the saints, to describe acts of virtue, and to relate biblical stories.

In modern times, Diego Rivera (1886-1957) revived this technique when he rendered large frescoes on public buildings in Mexico. Vigil (1947-) has been prolific in rendering the medium of fresco with murals of religious subjects, such as the *Pietá, San Pedro*, and *San Antonio*, for churches and schools, mostly in New Mexico. Balma (1957-) has created at the University of St. Thomas in Minneapolis fresco paintings depicting symbolism of the Seven Virtues. See Mural, Sistine Chapel, and Wall Painting.

Frottage (the art of disarrangement)

The placing of paper or canvas on a textured surface and then rubbing the paper or canvas with a crayon, pencil, or a paint-coated roller to get an impression. Thereafter, the artist amplifies and elaborates the forms seen in the texture by drawing or painting on it.

Although this art form was invented by the Chinese c. 350 B.C., the artist Ernst (1891-1976) coined the term "frottage." He used this technique in the creation of a series titled *Natural History*.

Stuart (1940-) became known for "earth scrolls" in the 1970s when she pounded, crushed, and rubbed earth and rocks onto muslin-backed paper: the earth became both medium and subject matter.

Functionalism

The belief that form should be based on function, especially in the decorative arts and architecture, but in the hope of producing something possessing beauty.

Funeral Monuments

These express better than anything else the attitude toward life and death, especially as seen during the Gothic period. In these monuments a statue of the deceased person may be lying on the coffin or posed in certain activities such as reading or praying. The figure would be dressed according to the position attained in life. One recurring theme of decoration was that of mourners dressed in robes and dramatically posed. Other themes were those of the sacred. See Sarcophagus.

Funk Art or Sick Art (late 1950s-1960s)

A group of artists in California who produced artworks combining the elements of Dada and Pop art; bizarre and macabre effects resulted.

Futurism (1909-1944)

A symbolic, noisy, political concept, rather than a movement, initiated by the Italian poet F. Marinetti with his manifesto declaring the end of art of the past and the birth of art of the future, an impulse that was adopted by poets, musicians, and politicians as well. They rejected all forms of realism or naturalism, believed that all things change rapidly, and theorized that all movement around, as well as space near and far, must be studied as part of "universal dynamism." The artists sought to blend their technique of color divisionism with the principles of Cubism. Boccioni (1882-1916), as the principal theorist, expressed its basic motifs: energy, light, movement, metropolis, and the dynamics of modern life.

Balla (1871-1958)	Russolo (1885-1947)
Carrá (1881-1966)	de Chirico (1888-1978)
Severini (1883-1966)	Bragagalia (1890-1960)

The second or synthetic phase of Futurism, known as Second Futurism, dating from 1915, consisted of the creation of three-dimensional works made from a variety of unconventional materials.

By 1918/1919 mechanistic themes and forms emerged. The artists believed the spirit of the machine should be rendered in accordance with "an original lyricism and not a preexisting scientific law."

At the end of the 1920s Aeropittura, with themes of flight and fantasy, became popular. Prampolini (1894-1956), its leading exponent, stated: "We need to transcend . . . and launch ourselves towards . . . a new world of cosmic reality."

The second phase of Aeropittura was represented by realistic paintings of planes in flight, aerial views, and the like.

From 1934 to 1944 (the year of Marinetti's death), Futurism had become a force in the disciplines of architecture, design, interiors, the decorative arts, the graphic arts, and banquets, all the while maintaining a radical, political stance. See Metaphysical School.

G

Gallery Copy

See Copy.

General Idea (1970s-1980s)

A Canadian movement that became internationally active. The artists worked in painting, sculpture, photography, film, video, and installations; they published the magazine *File,* an art-world caricature of *Life* magazine.

Their multimedia works were concerned with comical exposures of consumerism, along with appropriation of corporate logos and brand names. One of their most well-known works is the logo AIDS, based on Indiana's *Love* series. See Dada and Fluxus.

Genre (kind, type)

The depiction of actual, not ideal, scenes from ordinary life, recording everyman's history. Genre painters paint what they see. Their paintings are usually characteristic of a certain time, place, or other condition. Johnson (1824-1906) and Homer (1836-1910) are particularly known for genre scenes of American life.

Genre Figure

Referring to a small carved or molded statuette depicting a certain social class or group.

Geometric Abstraction

A style that combines simple geometric form with pure, simplified color, evenly applied. Its most common motifs are nonobjectivity, harmony, and reference to something with a supernatural or religious connotation.

Kupka (1871-1957) and Malevich (1878-1935) are recognized as painters of its first most severe representations; classic is Malevich's *Suprematist Elements: Two Squares.* See De Stijl, Hard-Edge Painting, Post-Painterly Abstraction, Purism, and Suprematism.

Geometric Form

Relating to simple forms such as the circle, square, and ovoid. They have been used frequently as allegorical symbols to allude to the mysteries of life.

Geometric Style

1. An art based on geometric form.
2. A primitive style used by ancient Greeks when they portrayed severely stylized figuration in vase painting.

German Expressionism

An extension of Fauve painting: the artists used explosive, aggressive color and primitivism. The belief that "art depends on inspiration, not technique" can be seen in works that ignore all academic teachings. Highly imaginative artworks are emotionally charged; the work of van Gogh (1853-1890) was the single greatest influence. By 1913, Expressionism was so widespread it was regarded as a German art form. See Bridge, New Artists' Association, and Blue Rider.

German School

Witz (1400-1445)
Lochner (1400-1451)
Schongauer (1430-1491)
Wolgemut (1434-1519)
Pacher (1435-1498)
Dürer (1471-1528)
Cranach (1472-1553)
Burgkmair (1473-1531)
Grünewald (1475-1528)
Breu (1475-1537)
Altdorfer (1480-1538)
Deutsch (1484-1530)
Baldung-Grien (1484-1545)
Huber (1490-1553)
Bruyn (1493-1555)
Holbein the Younger (1497-1543)
Beham (1500-1550)
Elsheimer (1578-1610)

Gesso

A fine plaster often used to prime a canvas so that the surface is ready to be painted. It imparts a distinctly characteristic quality to colors painted over it. See Ground.

Gesture Drawings

Referring to quickly drawn renderings of the movement of a figure or an object in space. Whatever the manner or material used, it is generally employed as a way to begin a composition, and constitutes the artist's understanding of a subject's form.

Giotteschi

A name given to describe the followers, pupils, and associates of Giotto (1266-1336). His followers signed themselves as "disciple of Giotto, the good master." See Gothic.

Giverny Group (1885-1920)

Referring to American artists who were strongly influenced by Monet and who lived temporarily near his home/studio in France, where American Impressionism was born.

In 1992, the Museum of American Art was built to house the artworks of the American Monet Circle in Giverny.

Glass Sculpture or Art Glass

The earliest known glass was made in Mesopotamia c. 2500 B.C. when small objects were crafted to imitate precious stones. After the Romans developed glassblowing, glass became common. While it is not precious in itself, artisans and craftspersons have used it to create many treasured objects, especially during the Greek/Hellenistic period and during the Middle Ages in Islam and in Europe. Beginning in the 1400s, the craft of glassblowing was passed on from father to son in Italy, and it wasn't until the 1600s that the first book of instructions for making glass was printed in Europe.

The era of Art Nouveau saw the creation of a new style of decoration, especially as seen in the hands of the Tiffany Furnaces, Steuben Glass Works, and other well-known glass-artwork manufacturers.

The Studio-Glass Movement, born in Ohio in 1962, encouraged the development of individual glassmakers, which led to the recognition of glass sculpture as a new art form: glassmakers started thinking of themselves as artists rather than craftspersons and their works became more sculptural and less utilitarian.

Pilchuck Glass School, located near Seattle and founded by the glass sculptor Chihuly in 1971, is now regarded as the most important glassblowing school in the world. Since 1991, Urban Glass in Brooklyn has dedicated itself as a place where artists create and teachers teach the craft of glassblowing. In recent years, cold-glass sculpture has led to a new flowering of artistic expression.

An increasing number of mainstream artists are now using glass as a medium for their artistry. Works by studio-glass movement leaders today fetch tens of thousands of dollars. See Art Nouveau and Stained Glass.

Glazing

A color effect made by applying a somewhat darker, transparent layer of color over a dry, lighter-colored layer. The purpose of glazing is simply to make two color layers optically blend. It also affords a tremendous flexibility in developing color nuances.

Golden Age of Dutch Manuscript Painting (late 1300s-1520)

These miniature illuminations depict fantasy, landscapes, interiors, idealized courtly scenes, and biblical tales, all rendered with exquisite brushwork and freedom of design. Outstanding is the Book of Hours attributed to the Master of Catherine of Cleves. See International Gothic.

Golden Age of Dutch Painting (1600s)

An age during the Baroque period that was witness to the emergence of many great artists. Rembrandt is recognized as the master of this age.

Portraits, landscapes, still lifes, interiors, town views, seascapes, and scenes of everyday life were introduced into the artistic lexicon and remained an integral part of Western painting until the 20th century. See Dutch School.

Golden Age of English Art (1700s)

An age which produced a number of master artists, namely, Constable, Gainsborough, Reynolds, and Turner. See English School.

Golden Age of German Painting

A period between the 14th and 16th centuries when many "Old German" masters (including those of Austria and Switzerland) and universal painters, such as Dürer, Grünewald and others of the German School, became known for the richness of their artistry.

Golden Age of Spain (1580-1680)

A time when Spain's empire included parts of Europe and the Americas. Under the encouragement of Spanish monarchs and through European connections, the Golden Age in the arts began. Writing, theatre, and the fine arts were basically extensions of the religious ideals and mystical nature of the Spanish people.

Golden Section or Golden Mean

A classical formula used to establish the relationship of parts to the whole: the rhythmic center of a composition is worked out with mathematical precision.

Gothic (1140-1400)

Gothic refers more to the architectural and sculptural arts rather than to painting. In sculptural form, religious beliefs and doctrines were illustrated. Early Gothic pictorial arts were represented by abstract and iconographical "painting with glass," panel painting, frescoes, and manuscript illumination.

The 12th and 13th centuries are known as the Age of Great Cathedrals, especially in France where about 580 large churches and cathedrals were built between 1178 and 1275. Chartres Cathedral is probably the finest example: its sculpture and stained glass, containing 8,000 images, represent the summation of Christian history. Continuity between the Old and New Testaments is manifested by allegory, realism, and symbolism.

During the late 1200s/early 1300s (Dugento and Trecento), aspects of the modern world began to be manifested in the work of Cimabue (1240-1302) and Cavallini (1250-1330).

With the aid of Byzantine theories, Giotto (1266-1336) of the Florentine School rediscovered the Greek method of creating the illusion of depth. He was the first to connect dramatic events with living persons, and the first to give movement and to express emotion. He was recognized as a master who led to a true revival of art and who changed the whole idea of painting. At the same time, Duccio (1260-1319) of the Sienese School was successful in breathing new life into old Byzantine forms. He was among the first to create paintings based on nature. Both Giotto and Duccio had numerous followers.

The Effects of Good Government in the City and the Country (46 x 8 ft.) by A. Lorenzetti (active 1319-1348) is evidence of a humanist trend. It was the first attempt to show a real place in a real setting with real inhabitants: the streets and shops of Siena along with a patchwork of fields. This painting may well be the first panoramic landscape of the Western world.

The term "Late Gothic" is ascribed to artists in Northern Europe, who were the counterparts of the Early Renaissance — most notably the Master of Flémalle (1378-1444), one of the first artists to use oil paint, and Jan van Eyck (1385-1441) and his brother Hubert (d. 1426), who perfected the technique of oil painting. The brothers van Eyck probably produced the greatest masterpiece of Flemish painting with *The Ghent Altarpiece*. See Flemish School.

In Germany, sculpture forged ahead in an expressive and realistic manner. German Gothic also flourished in the form of manuscript illumination.

English Gothic is particularly manifest in the Lincoln Cathedral and Westminster Abbey and, later in the Gothic period, in styles called the Decorated Style and the

Perpendicular Style.

Spanish Gothic is seen in the mastery of small-scale sculpture.

In sum, Gothic art brought the trends of Northern Europe to a brilliant climax. The traditions of Southern Europe were absorbed in a new and original style. Through Catholic Christendom and monastic orders, the Gothic style was spread throughout Europe.

The concluding phase of Gothic is known as International Gothic, with its origins in the French courts.

Gothic is magnificently extant in the New World: the Cathedral of the Sacred Heart in Newark, New Jersey, and the Sacred Heart Church at Notre Dame University, among others. See Humanism, Northern European Art, and Renaissance.

Gouache

A watercolor mixed with white to obtain an opaque effect. Its chief advantage is the ease with which it can be handled, making it comparable to oil paint in rendering meticulous detail. It is also known for the beauty of its mat finish and bright color effects.

This medium was used especially by illuminators of medieval manuscripts and was common in Indian, Persian, and Turkish miniature painting: portraiture and narrative with religious, historical, and romantic themes.

Gouache is popular today as an alternative to pure watercolor.

Graffito

Referring to incised decoration of centuries past: the application of layers of plaster upon which a design was then scratched through the top layer while still damp. There are prehistoric examples of its graphic use in caves. In today's world, the term "graffiti" is used to describe uninvited drawings and scribblings sprayed on buildings and public transit by vandals. There has developed a style, however, which imitates graffiti, but is painted or sprayed on canvas or commissioned spaces. Classic is the work of Haring (1958-1990) and Basquiat (1960-1988). See Post-Pop Art.

Grand Manner/Style

1. An elevated style of history painting showing heroic figures in idealized settings. In academic theory, the grand manner was the only way to treat lofty themes from the Bible or from history and mythology.
2. The communication of truth, morality, or spiritual values through paintings with allegorical, historical, or sacred themes.

Graphic Arts

Basically, the arts of drawing and printmaking. Various media are used and, in its broadest sense, it can apply to anything that is linear; specifically, it refers to various print processes.

The earliest woodcut (relief print) was developed in China. By the 1400s, when paper was manufactured and printing was introduced, the woodcut was established in Europe. Next in appearance were playing cards and block-books.

Many technical problems were overcome by the skills of Altdorfer, Dürer, and

Schongauer of the German School. Rembrandt of the Dutch School is credited with introducing the modern view that the graphic arts can be used as a means of expression.

The Japanese color woodcut was a strong influence on many artists of the School of Paris. See Ukiyo-e. The work of Toulouse-Lautrec has been one of the major sources of modern developments in the graphic arts.

Some forms of graphic art, such as drawing, engraving, etching, and lithography, are classified as fine arts, while other processes, such as typography and printing, have a functional quality. Well-known types of graphic art include:

A. Intaglio (cutting below the surface): Engraving, etching, mezzotint, and aquatint.
B. Relief (uneven surface): Woodcut, photoengraving, and linocut.
C. Planograph (surface): Lithography, monotype or décalcomania, and photographic methods.
D. Stencil (pochoir): Silk-screen/serigraph.

This listing is not inclusive. See Poster, Print, Printmaking, and Repligraphy.

Graphic Design

A term coined by W.A. Diggins in 1922. This applied art reduces ideas or messages to unique signs and symbols. In essence, logos and icons have been created to capture the memory of a populace and are identifiable with a vernacular culture. See Semiotics.

Great Paintings

Paintings by Church (1826-1900), titled *Niagara, The Heart of the Andes*, *Twilight in the Wilderness*, and *New England Scenery*, helped elevate the visual arts to a new status in the US. Terms such as "sublime," "truthful," and "religious" were used to describe these artworks that glorify the luminous and the spiritual in nature. See Hudson River School.

Greek Art

The Greeks made no real distinction between arts and crafts. Its known historic periods include:

1. Protogeometric (1000-900 B.C.)
   The Mycenaean influence of arcs and circles is seen on vases; the Greek style, however, is superior and the painted decoration more skillful.

2. Geometric (900-725 B.C.)
   The decoration of vases and small-scale sculpture had by now developed new patterns alongside older ones. The most common designs were meanders, zigzags, and triangles. These abstractions, together with human and animal figuration, were all done within a geometric framework.

3. Archaic (725-480 B.C.)
   Eastern forms and techniques were adopted and soon mastered by the Greeks. In form and substance, the Eastern influence consisted of work in the mediums of bronze and ivory in creating small sculptures. The biggest influence was that of vase painting; floral devices and new outline drawing (black figures with incised details) were the motifs. It was a vital period and vase painters

were held in high esteem: they were called "Little Masters." (Because vase painting depicts almost the whole range of stories and images that interested the Greeks, much of the world's knowledge about Greek civilization, culture, and mythology is derived from this art form.)

The Egyptian influence is seen in stone statuary and architecture; a unity of scale developed. Relief was used on gravestones to depict scenes or portraits. Red-figure vase painting in detail became popular. See Kouros.

4. Classical (also called The Golden Age of Athens) (480-323 B.C.)

   This period reflects the highest point of Greek ideals and established the principles of Classical art. One of its manifestations was a great sense of proportion. Sculpture in white marble was mostly in the round; it was also commonly used in relief for ornamentation of friezes.

   In architecture, the Parthenon most likely possessed the most perfect exterior the world had ever seen: its sculpture demonstrated the fullest expression of Greek ideals with human figuration represented in its prime. The Parthenon took 15 years to build; in later ages it was used as a church, a mosque, and a powder magazine.

   A major step forward was the discovery of the technique of bronze casting. (The Chinese had invented it c. 1700 B.C.) Portraiture was important; mosaics and mural- and panel-painting are known through literature to have been popular. Minor arts included the making of coins, jewelry, weapons, and utensils.

5. Hellenistic (323-31 B.C.)

   After the death of Alexander, a change occurred: statuary commemorated events and honored personifications, deities, and members of royal families. There was a greater closeness to everyday events; naturalism, rather than idealism, prevailed. Jewelry and artifacts became finer and more decorative; vase painting declined.

   Some works of classical sculpture which have enjoyed the greatest fame, however, were created during this period. It was at this time that people of wealth started to collect original artworks or their copies and to pay high prices for them.

   In sum, the Greeks used their own eyes and experimented in the creation of art to render natural forms through shading, expression, and movement; the Egyptians used only their knowledge of art. Myron, in his execution of the sculpture *Discus Thrower* (c. 450 B.C.) is credited with conquering movement; other Greeks were able to master space.

   Although artists were still looked upon as craftspersons, between 520-420 B.C. an interest in art for its own sake developed and comparisons were made between various schools. (Approximately 2500 years ago, individual artistic achievement was not commonly known: the work of only a few Greek masters was attributed.)

   Basic to Greek thought was its intense preoccupation with man and its striving for rational interpretation. This interest in man found visual expression in sculpture. Generally speaking, the Greeks were masters of architecture and sculpture and they excelled in painting.

Grisaille

1. A monochromatic painting, executed in gray shades, that appears sculptural—a popular technique in medieval painting.
2. In late Middle Ages, a technique in which enamel drawings were executed on plain glass.
3. Underpainting in gray tones to establish form.

Ground

1. A coating of primer applied to a support to prepare the surface for painting; also, the background.
2. In sculpture, the surface from which a figure projects.

As a note to history, the Dutch artist Hals (1580-1666) was one of the pioneers of the technique in which paint is applied directly to the support without underpainting.

Groupe de Recherche d'Art Visuel (GRAV) (1959-1960s)

A group of Parisian artists who researched and experimented together in the categories of light, movement, and vision. Mechanisms and illusion were the motifs. One of the group's aims was to reduce art to "a simple activity of man" by redirecting "the function of the eye toward a new visual situation." Many of the works were titled *Instability*. Le Parc (1928-   ) was the group's founder. See Audiokinetic Sculpture.

Group of Seven (1920s-1930s)

The first important national movement in Canada. Like the Hudson River School, the artists took pride in painting the countryside and the wilderness of their country: the policy was "to encourage and foster the growth of art . . . which has a national character." (In 1933, the artists changed the group's name to "Canadian Group of Painters.")

Grupo/Collectiva

A term that defines a group of Mexican artists working in different media, but with similar goals, and operating mostly in public or non-specialized spaces. This concept flourished in Mexico City in the 1970s. The term has been extended to Chicano artists working in California.

Gruppe-D

A popular, contemporary, informal collective of German painters, sculptors, ceramicists, and graphic artists whose artworks refer indirectly to the atrocities committed by the Nazis during the Holocaust. Their home base is Dachau, one of the most active art communities in Germany.

Gúeridons (small, round tables)

A series of Cubist paintings rendered by Braque (1882-1963). Ever present in the paintings are a guitar, clay pipe, fruit bowl, and musical instruments.

Guerrilla Action (1990s)

A group of artists in New Jersey whose principal theme is that art should be thought-provoking. Their attention-getting actions and stunts focus on the AIDS crisis, war, censorship, advertising, homeless society, and other social problems.

Guerrilla Girls (1980s-1990s)

An anonymous group of artists in New York City masquerading in gorilla masks. Their aim is to protest the seemingly sexist attitude of art dealers and curators who underrepresent women artists. Their modus operandi is to plaster posters in public places during midnight "raids," which contain lists of grievances against the male-dominated art world, as well as the names of those they accuse of perpetuating discrimination against female artists. In the 1990s, they have reached out to other cities.

As a note to history, during centuries past artworks of many female artists were attributed to their male relatives or teachers on the assumption that no first-class art could have been produced by a woman. It was not until the mid-1500s, in Italy, that female artists with major international reputations emerged; nevertheless, women have been denied equal status with their male counterparts well into the 20th century.

Guild

In medieval Europe, most tradespeople and artisans, including artists, belonged to a guild. Important cities organized their own guilds for artists; proof of mastery of his craft by the artist was necessary to gain membership. The artist was then permitted to open a workshop, employ apprentices, and to accept commissions. These guilds were usually wealthy, politically active, and eager to make their respective cities prosperous and beautiful.

Women were not admitted to the guilds, nor to workshops, studios or academies where artists were trained.

Gutai Group (1954-1972)

A group of Japanese painters of the Art Informel School, who adopted abstraction and instinctive, spontaneous creation as their technique. They were also known for Happenings.

H

Haggadah

In Jewish book art, it depicts the rituals for domestic services on holy days. Preceding pages of the subject matter of the volume contain pictures of biblical history.

Hague School (c.1860-1900)

A group of Dutch artists whose paintings portray scenes from everyday life, including beach and street scenes, church interiors, and landscapes. Their romantic renderings reflect the effects of light and atmospheric conditions.

Haida Art

The art of native peoples who lived approximately 1,000 years ago on islands south of Alaska. They were recognized as accomplished carvers and the best canoe builders. Ordinary carved implements and ceremonial artifacts suggest the faces and bodies of familiar and mythic creatures.

Davidson (1946-) paints Haida representations on deerskin and sculpts totem poles. He said: "The Haida believe everything is human. In . . . the supernatural world, creatures look human."

Half-Tone Process

An invention in 1878 which made possible the reproduction of monochromatic photographs, paintings, or drawings used for newspapers, journals, art books, and periodicals. It meant the end of employment for large art staffs on such publications.

Hand of the Artist

Referring to the artist's brushwork as evidence of the artist's hand and mark of personal identity. See Brushwork and Signature Style.

Happening

A term especially associated with the activities of a group of artists in New York City during the late 1950s and the 1960s. Generally, it defines an abstract event that ordinarily takes place only once and, although there may be a script, there is no dialog, no logical sequence of events and, in large part, details of its execution are left up to the artist: a kind of "sculpture in action" when things are made to happen. Its aim: to increase awareness of the connection between art and life and to raise human consciousness. See Conceptual Art, Fluxus, Performance Art, and Process Art.

Hard-Edge Painting

A term coined by the critic J. Langsner in 1958 to replace the term "Geometric Abstraction." The artists divided the canvas into clearly defined edges and rigid forms that were delineated with flat planes of color. See *Homage to the Square* and Post-Painterly Abstraction.

Harlem Renaissance (1920s-early 1930s)

The flowering of black art and literature in the US: the cradle of contemporary black culture, including the presence of exceptional dancers, singers and musicians. These years heralded an almost overwhelming outpouring of artistic talent. It was a time when many artists turned their attention to black American subject matter and created images with a distinctively ethnic quality.

More recently, a new black cultural renaissance seems to have been born because of an astonishing burst of activity in the fields of writing, music, art, and dance. See Black American Art.

Harmony

The blending of tone, color, and line to bring about balance; something pleasing to the eye.

Heraldry

Decorative art using armorial insignia or emblems. The adoption of symbols of identification by families, tribes, and nations is an ancient, universal tradition. By the 1500s, this tradition declined when surnames were adopted. In the Native American culture, totem poles are used to identify tribes.

Hermitage

Located in St. Petersburg, it is the world's largest museum with 354 rooms in five 18th-century palaces, but with only enough space to exhibit a fraction of its artworks. Its collection contains millions of artworks from all ages and from many countries; it constitutes one of the great collections of Western art from Old Masters to early modernism. See Museum.

As a note to history, during WWII curators moved artworks to the bombproof cellars and packed the rest for evacuation. Throughout the duration of the German siege, 2,000 starving conservators and artists lived in the underground storerooms. Although half of the population of St. Petersburg (then called Leningrad) died because of the war, artworks in the Hermitage cellars survived.

High Art

Referring to art created in the classical or traditional, academic style.

High Renaissance (1500-1580)

The second phase of the Renaissance when symmetry and the recapture of classical antiquity reached full expression with completion of the Sistine Chapel and the Vatican frescoes. The various works of Leonardo da Vinci (1452-1519), Michelangelo (1475-1564), and Raphael (1483-1520) were glorified. Bramante (1444-1514) was the creator of High Renaissance architecture. By this time, the artist was seen as a supreme genius, which spurred him to inspired goals.

In general, artists provided a new level of technical mastery: those who followed were able to create works of unheard-of dramatic power.

Painting reached its zenith in Venice, a latecomer to the Renaissance, with the work of Gentile Bellini (1429-1507), Giovanni Bellini (1430-1516), and Carpaccio (1465-1526).

The work of Titian (1490-1576) probably represents the highlight of the Venetian School.

In sum, by 1500 painters, sculptors, and architects had created a new aesthetic and a new vision of the purpose of art. See Mannerism.

Hispanic Art in the U.S.

The term "Hispanic art" is relatively new. The first time it caught the public's attention was in the late 1960s when Chicano movements in California campaigned for civil rights with large murals containing political or historical themes. "Los Four" thereafter continued the tradition of large paintings of Chicano history and barrio culture in Los Angeles.

Other Hispanic artists, who have their roots in the US, Europe, or Latin America, have painted and sculpted a great variety of subjects, with some emphasis on religious themes. Several artists fused Southwestern imagery with Chicanismo. Sculptures characterize well-known types of that region (the cowboy and the pioneer), while landscape pictures reflect on life in the Southwest.

Representational art has always dominated Hispanic art, but it has been rendered in diverse ways such as graffiti and cartoon art.

As more painters and sculptors come to the US, they bring with them their traditional themes and styles which meld into their new cultural environment. See Mujeres Muralistas.

History Painting

Referring to grand pictures with allegorical, biblical, historical, or mythological narrative, once regarded by academies as the highest and most proper form of art.

LeMoyne (d. 1588), a French explorer-artist, rendered *First Painting of America-Florida, 1564*, which may well be the first American-history painting. The paintings of John White (active 1584-1593) during English expeditions into the New World are vivid recollections of Native American life before the coming of the white man.

Other painters of historic scenes or events in the US include:

Pine (1730-1788)
Copley (1738-1815)
West (1738-1820), the father of American-history painting
J. Peale (1749-1831)
Trumbull (1756-1843)
H. Sargent (1770-1845)
Morse (1791-1872)
Weir (1803-1889)
Stearns (1810-1885)
Leutze (1816-1868)
Thompson (1840-1896)
MacKenzie (1865-1941)

See Early American Art, National Work, Revolutionary Art, Tableau d'Histoire, and War Art.

Holography

Photographs taken with laser beams which produce three-dimensional images behind or in front of a transparent or reflective surface. Viewing is possible from all angles. See $(ART)^n$.

Homage to the Square

Albers (1888-1976), a colorist, theorized every color was affected by the color next to it. His lifelong interest was to make colors do something they don't do by themselves. He proved this theory with a series of paintings in which he used a simple square-within-a-square format.

Hoosier School/Group

A group of Impressionist painters in Indiana who became known as a cultural force when their paintings were exhibited at the Columbian Exposition of 1893. They are now regarded as one of the leading groups of American Impressionist landscape painters.

Hudson River School (1820s-1880s)

A group of artists who may represent the first American movement. They specialized in the grandeur of landscape and luminism. The origin of their art lay in romantic literature; they were proud to be pioneers in showing America's vast, natural, and unspoiled beauty.

Cole (1801-1848), a spokesperson for the first generation, urged that artists sketch country scenes in open air.

One of the leaders of the second generation, Durand (1796-1886), is known as the father of American landscape painting. These artists tended to be more realistic when they copied nature by making careful drawings of details and presenting light in a more natural manner. (Durand's belief that an artist who painted a landscape faithful to God's divine work, thereby creating a visual sermon to uplift man, led to the popularity of the Hudson River School.)

The third generation adopted loose brushwork in an attempt to capture the mood of the scene.

Artists who found their inspiration in the West are known as the Rocky Mountain School, most notably Bierstadt (1830-1902) and Moran (1837-1926). Panoramic landscapes rendered by these artists inspired the government to preserve areas of extraordinary beauty as national parks. See American Landscape, American Tonalism, Taos/Santa Fe School, and White Mountain Painters.

Human Concretion

A term used by Arp (1887-1966) to describe his organic sculptures. He said: "Concretion is something that has grown." See Biomorphic Abstraction.

Humanism

A popular theory during the Renaissance, which resulted in the gradual introduction of nonreligious themes into art. It was not anti-religion. The term was adopted from the Greek and the Latin to refer to those studies that are worthy of the dignity of man such as literature, language, and philosophy. Emphasis in education circles was on classical studies, the study of antiquity.

Basically, the theory conceived that man could be his own master through study and research and that all philosophical and religious ideas should be thought out.

Humanism also advanced the growth of personalities, as opposed to past anonymity in art, and played an important role in the development of art theory.

Hyper-Realism

In Modern art, the depiction of anything general—a cocktail party, a drugstore window—in photographic reality. The effect may be that of lifeless emptiness. See Photo-Realism.

I

Icon

A representation of a sacred person/scene used in Eastern churches, originating from Early Christian and Byzantine sources, and usually painted on wood panels. In modern usage, a symbolic image.

Iconography

The symbolism or imagery of a body of art to express universal ideas: a collection of pictures representing a visual record.

Ideal Art

An art based on aesthetic ideals. It grew out of the Greek classical style with emphasis on a perfectly proportioned figure. This style remained popular until the 1800s.

Illumination (to light up)

The art of decorating manuscripts with small designs, scenes, and portraits of the author, including elegant calligraphy whereby the initial letters and opening phrases are enlarged. The illuminations were usually executed in pen and ink or in brilliantly colored gouache, frequently highlighted with gold leaf. See Fraktur, Haggadah, Manuscript Illumination, and Miniature Painting.

Illusionism

The use of various devices, such as modeling, perspective, or proportion, to create the appearance of reality.

Illusionistic Painting

Most painting of the Western world from the period of the Renaissance until the advent of Modern art was illusionistic in that subjects appear as though in the real world, through the use of space or perspective. See Allusive Painting.

Illustration

The artistic interpretation of an idea, scene, or writing, used to enhance the meaning of a text in books, magazines, and posters.

Illustrator

An artist who is able to capture and interpret the essence of a story and whose work is usually regarded as unique and original. Illustrators were a great tradition in American art and many of them were well known and well liked, especially those who illustrated for popular magazines.

They continue to flourish. (As a note to history, the Golden Age of Illustration in the US had its beginnings in the 1880s.)

Hughes (1832-1915)
Homer (1836-1910)
Abbey (1852-1911)
Pyle (1853-1911)
Sterner (1863-1957)
Parrish (1870-1966)
Leyendecker (1874-1951)
N.C. Wyeth (1882-1945)
Kent (1882-1971)
Rockwell (1894-1978)
Vargas (1896-1984)
Sundblom (1899-1976)
Stahl (1910-1987)
Peak (1928-1992)
Marshall (1942-1992)
Botas (1958-1992)

Imagery

A collection of forms within an artwork giving expression to the artist's ideas. In Abstract art, the forms and shapes perceived by the artist.

Imaginative Paintings

A term coined by Pelton (1881-1961) for her symbolist compositions, with the human form used as a vehicle for poetic and philosophical ideas.

Impasto

The thick application of paint which often adds character and energy to a painting. Also, the raised decoration on ceramicware. See Knife Work and Palette Knife.

Impressionism

A painterly style of painting with its seed first planted by the Barbizon School. It was a unified movement by 1874 and exhibitions were held eight times, from that year until 1886.

The Impressionists saw the world subjectively and intuitively, according to the sensations of light and movement. They were aware that color changed under light and, in interpreting the play of light, the subject became secondary. Emphasis was placed on painting everyday scenes, in contrast to traditional subjects favored by academicians: a new vision was pioneered when the artists depicted the naturalistic world around them. Their favorite subjects were radiant landscapes and picnics, boating scenes, race tracks, balls, music halls, cafe concerts, and portraiture: the celebration of life and leisure. These attributes, taken together with the fact that Impressionists eliminated the most important academic standards of technique, finish, and composition, represented a whole reevaluation of art. Perhaps their greatest achievements were the sensation of liveliness, the liberation of pure, bright colors, freedom of the brushstroke, and the use of a natural optical mixture technique when they introduced the concept of complementary colors, especially in the rendition of shadow which they painted in color.

Academic painters of other countries were strongly influenced by the new style; it is now regarded as the most popular movement in Western art.

Monet (1840-1926) is known as the father of Impressionism; he made hourly studies of the same subject in which the quality of shadow and light was analyzed. Classic is the *Cathedral* series.

C. Pissarro (1830-1903)
Sisley (1839-1899)
Bazille (1841-1870)
Morisot (1841-1895)
Renoir (1841-1919)
Cassatt (1845-1926)
Caillebotte (1848-1894)
Gonzalés (1849-1883)

See American Impressionism, Intimist Painters, Macchiaioli School, and Neo-Impressionism.

Improvisations (1910-1913)

A series of 40 abstract paintings rendered by Kandinsky (1866-1944). He attempted to reconcile his nonobjective paintings with supernatural or musical symbols.

Incunabula

Referring to books printed just after the invention of movable type (c. 1400) until 1500. These early printed books looked like manuscripts: spaces were left for initials and illustrations added by hand. See Manuscript Illumunation.

Independent Artists, Exhibition of (1910)

The first exhibition in the US without any conditions or prerequisites placed on the artists. It was organized by Henri (1865-1929) and Sloan (1871-1951) to provide opportunities for young artists. This exhibition formed an important link between exhibitions of The Eight and the Armory Show.

Independent Artists, Society of (1917-1941)

This society was formed in New York City for the purpose of creating outlets for modern artists. Its exhibitions were modeled on the French annual Salon des Indépendants: no jury and no prizes. The first exhibition had the work of over 1100 artists represented. Traveling exhibitions and regional shows were encouraged.

Indian Art (500s B.C. - A.D. 1000)

Stonework, metalwork, and painting were the major art forms of this culture and were basically related to the themes of sex and religion in harmonious combination. India has produced numerous styles of painting, sculpture, and architecture. Sculpture, however, in the form of carvings, reliefs, and free-standing figures, played a vital role. The main difference between temples of various religions was reflected in the sculptures adorning them.

The heart of Hinduism is revelation that is described in poetic metaphors and symbols. The creation of Hindu art was the result of the unison of social and religious groups. It was the belief that every natural being has a spirit which can be invoked by ritual to become visible. Stonework in the form of statues — at first colossal in size, but diminishing in size through the centuries — were essentially iconographic images. A statue with multiple arms symbolized the various powers of that image. The earliest wall painting from A.D. 500 was found in a cave dedicated to the god Vishnu; mural paintings from the 8th/9th centuries were found in various cave-shrines and temples. Persian techniques in miniature size were introduced by the Muslims, with themes taken from religious stories, myths, and epics: woman was commonly the central character.

The Buddhist religion was dominated by architecture, relief sculpture, and painting. Ritual cave-shrines from A.D. 200-700 contain non-fresco wall paintings depicting religious rituals, stories from Buddha's previous lives, and scenes from everyday life.

The Jaina religion believed in a series of saviors, each of which was reproduced in iconographic statues. A marble ceiling containing hundreds of sculpted forms representing gods, their attendants, flowers, etc., created in the 11th century in the Vimala Shah temple, is classic of its iconography. Rock-art architecture was modeled on Buddhist work.

From A.D. 1000 to 1500, various dynasties built magnificent temples in an effort to outdo one another. Regional differences became more defined, but sculpture and architecture remained closely associated. Muslim invasions caused a decline in the quality and tradition of art. It was not until the Mughal Dynasty, under the influence of Europeanism, that art became richer. After the 1700s, artists became mere copiers, rather than originators.

Indian Arts and Crafts Act (1990)

In essence, this act states a Native American must prove tribal membership in order to exhibit his/her artworks as true American Indian creations. This has caused a dilemma because many Native Americans' parents/grandparents did not register with recognized tribes, leaving their progeny with no certification. (Other reasons also exist for non-certification.) The act is the only such law that has been applied to any ethnic group in the US.

Indian Gallery (1837-1851)

The great American painter of Indians, Catlin (1796-1872), traveled throughout Europe for 14 years in an art/Wild West show in which he exhibited his gallery of portraits of Native Americans, landscapes, genre scenes, and religious ceremonies.

Catlin has been called "the first artist of the West" because of his lifelong devotion to the Western scene; he was a pioneer in portraying Native Americans as unique individuals. See *Sketches*.

Industrial Craft

The merging of state-of-the-art techniques: tradition, technology, handcraftsmanship, and computer-aided design produce high tech and high touch.

Industrial Design

The design and decoration of useful objects such as furniture and appliances. Its primary aim is the merging of new design ideas and new technology in the hope of generating sales.

The well-known designer D. Rams said: "Although a simple form is generally more difficult to develop . . . in the long run this is the best design."

Infilling

Following the sketch, infilling takes place when forms and colors are applied to the outlines.

Information Art

The term "information" is used in connection with beautiful, complex patterns created by a network of data flowing through integrated circuits. These circuits or microchips are now regarded as among the most highly designed and exquisitely crafted artifacts of today's civilization. Because of their aesthetic appeal, they are a strong influence in the work of textile artists, graphic artists, and painters.

Infra-Mince

A category invented by Duchamp (1887-1968), meaning "sub-tiny." It referred to wasted energy and was a reaction to the giant, opulent canvases of Modern art. It was Duchamp's intention that art should be so small as to be almost insignificant.

In Situ

The creation or repair of an artwork on the site for which it is intended. See Site-Specific Art.

Installation

A term used by curators and art dealers when preparing a new exhibition.

"Instant" Art

The Polaroid Corporation has devised a process whereby any two-dimensional image can be replicated in sizes up to 40 x 80 inches. This expensive process (over $1,000) captures the image in remarkably realistic detail.

International Art and Antique Loss Register

Modern-day sleuths have put together a new generation of computers to combat theft in the art world: optical disk technology to file photographs of lost/stolen art. The register's team of art historians type in descriptions of their own, plus data from several official sources; the computers then search the data base for images that match descriptions. See Artguard.

International Gothic or International Style (1375-1425)

During this period, the influence of French and Italianate art spread throughout Northern Europe. Ideas were transmitted by artists in their travels: a mutual exchange resulted. Naturalistic renderings of beautiful objects and the surrounding world were portrayed in illuminated manuscripts marked with elegance of form, curvilinear, harmonious line, delicate color, and a courtly style.

The brothers Limbourg (active 1399-1439) are probably the best-known artists of this period. See *Très Riches Heures*.

In the decorative arts, there was a booming production of tapestries, textiles, small sculptures, jewelry, portrait medallions, and other objects. See Renaissance.

International Museum of Children's Art

In 1986, perhaps the only museum of its kind opened in Oslo. It exhibits artworks created by children only.

In the Round

In full sculpted form: three dimensional.

Intimist Painters

Referring to the highly individual Post-Impressionists Bonnard (1867-1947) and Vuillard (1868-1940), who adapted some of the methods and colors of Impressionism to interior and close-up scenes of bourgeois life. The artists were fascinated with subtle variations of light and radiant, shimmering color. Juxtaposed pattern was the motif: the effects of warmth and intimacy resulted. See Nabis.

Isenheim Altarpiece (1510-1511)

A masterpiece executed by Grünewald of the German School. It consists of a polyptych of 11 parts and portrays the fundamental beliefs of the Christian religion. It is one of the great works of Northern European art and is classic of Teutonic imagery. See Altarpiece.

Islamic Art (600s-1600s)

It was not the art of any particular region or people because the Islamic religion did not identify itself in terms of nationality. Religion, therefore, was the uniting factor. In addition to monuments, mosques, and palaces decorated with wall paintings, tile, and plasterwork, art was generally represented by the use of rich color, arabesque, intricate pattern, calligraphy, and ornamentation — all bound within the spirit of religion.

Crafts included lacework, knotted rugs and carpets, metalwork, mosaics, glassware, ivory and wood carvings, and outstanding painted pottery, along with narrative relief and sculpture in the round for wall niches.

Manuscript painting was the major pictorial expression: the pictures portray a variety of themes such as hunting scenes, religious rites, romance, and legends. Islamic art known as Timurid painting, in particular that of the Herat School, reached full expression in the 1600s.

In sum, rather than creating original work, it was the artist's mastery of working within a standard set of conventions that was of prime importance. Muslim craftspersons continue in the crafts of metalwork, carpeting, textiles, etc.

Italianizers or Romanists (1500s-1600s)

Artists from the Low Countries who worked in the Italianate style.

J

Japanese Art

Its fundamentals:

1. Arts and crafts are related to each other with no real distinction made between them.
2. Presentation and appropriateness.
3. An intense feeling for nature: the recurring theme of the four seasons.
4. A tension between the high art of spirituality and the low art of rich living.

Its major tendencies:

1. Direct imitation of the world (as reflected by the Chinese style of the past 1200 years) and Western influence. Japan has always absorbed foreign influences; its primary models, however, were Chinese calligraphy, ceramics, and painting.
2. Poetic imagery whereby Japanese originality and tradition thrive with the expression of beauty, spirituality, and harmony.

Japan's contribution to the world of art:

1. The mastery of color prints. Those produced by the Edo School (1615-1867) through the graphic process of woodcuts were marked by bright colors, bold outlines, simplicity, and blank areas to create the impression of light. When the Japanese resumed trade relations with the West in the mid-1800s, colorful prints were exported as wrappings. These prints influenced many artists of the School of Paris. See Ukiyo-e.
2. The expressionism and realism of sculpture.
3. The craft of pottery continues to produce exciting work, along with lacquerwork, metalwork, and textiles. A major breakthrough in Western pottery design occurred when Westerners learned the expressive methods of Japanese design.

Beginning in 1868, Japan made westernization and modernization its twin goals. Students began studying in the West and foreigners established colleges and universities in Japan. In today's world, art is a vital force and, while artists are encouraged to learn new styles, their own traditions remain a living power.

Two useful terms: yohga, meaning Japanese Western-style painting; nihonga, meaning Japanese traditional painting.

Japonisme

The influence of Japanese art and design in the Western world.

Jewish Art

The beginning of art in the Jewish tradition was similar to that of other early cultures. In later centuries, elegant stone and earthenware crockery, ivory carvings, fine jewelry, stelas, and large painted compositions adorning houses were typical. The ancient Canaanites developed decorative motifs such as painted pottery and the *Tree of Life* with its complicated scrollwork.

The origin of the synagogue, the mother of the Christian church and the mosque, may have been during the "Babylonian exile." Its principal decoration evolving over the years was mosaic flooring, often depicting figuration. Jewish pictorial art emerged in the 3rd century A.D., as evidenced by frescoes in the Synagogue at Dura Europos. During excavations of catacombs in 1955, reliefs, graffiti, wall paintings, and stone coffins were discovered; a variety of Folk art emerged.

Art objects, especially during the Talmudic period, always bore some Jewish symbol or association: classic is the menorah. Glasswork ("gold-glass" dishes) and vessels made of metal and clay are known to have existed.

In the Middle Ages, gold-and silversmithery were characteristic of Jewish occupations. Brocades, lavishly decorated curtains for the tabernacle, and a large variety of objects (including majolica) connected with ceremonials became familiar artifacts. The illumination of Hebrew manuscripts during this period is best seen in the Farhi Bible, the Kennicott Bible, and in many Haggadahs created in various countries. This art form reached its zenith in Italian Jewish book illumination.

After the invention of printing, the main artistic activity was ornamentation of scrolls of the Book of Esther.

In the 1700s, the Germanic countries witnessed a renewal of book illumination. In the production of printed books, scribe illuminators were still called upon; well-known type-artist/cutters were employed to create beautiful lettering. See Calligraphy.

Many artists became known for portrait-engraving; they were known as miniaturists. During the emergence of modern Jewish art, miniature painting became popular; portraits were usually of Jewish personages.

In the 1800s, artists began to discover everyday Jewish scenes. The first group of painters who constituted a school or movement was located in The Hague in Holland, most notably the three Verveer brothers. German Jewish etchers and draftsmen in the late 1800s/early 1900s made outstanding contributions to the evolution of the graphic arts.

Jewish artists participated in all the modern movements such as the Barbizon School, the Macchiaioli School, the Impressionists, the Nabis, and so on. (The majority of these artists occasionally sought inspiration in Jewish ceremonials and in folklore.) They were active in every country among the great innovators; many were of the School of Paris, who were deported by the Nazis and killed. The tyranny of Stalin, under the aegis of Socialist Realism, eliminated or ousted many artists, including those who attempted to formulate a national Jewish style, most notably Chagall (1887-1985) and Ryback (1897-1935). Nevertheless, the period from the turn of the century until the breakup of the Soviet Union was one of outstanding achievement in the lives of Jewish artists, including those who were among innovators of new artistic styles.

A survey of the contribution to the fine arts by Jewish men and women, especially as adherents of avant-garde movements, would require a volume.

Junk Art and Sculpture

A term first applied to canvases which had attached to them rags, torn reproductions, and found objects. The term was extended to describe assemblages of abstract sculpture created from the detritus of machine civilization.

The Italian artist Ceni (1958-) uses paint, twine, oil, wire, and other everyday industrial products to reproduce and build on moments drawn from daily life.

Chamberlain (1927-) assembles crushed and crumpled parts of automobiles: bumpers, fenders, and doors are the raw material of junk sculpture. The artist's palette is the junkyard and the auto-repair shop.

Nouveau Réaliste artist César (1921-) created *Compressions* (squeezed car bodies) and *Reliefs* (wall pieces composed of colorful automobile car parts).

K

Kachina Dolls

These colorfully painted wooden effigies, carved by Pueblo Indians called Hopi, have been a popular form of Folk art for centuries. Initially, they were made from crude blocks, with painted-on clothing; gradually, they evolved into artworks adorned with distinguishing details of mask, costume, and color. To the Hopi, the dolls represent man/spirit and elemental forces in the visible world, and take many forms: demons, ogres, gods, animals, birds, or clowns.

In a Catholic Church (now a national landmark) located on the Zuni Indian Reservation in New Mexico, murals of some two dozen life-size kachinas have been painted in vibrant colors: summer rain dances, winter solstice celebrations, and other rituals are depicted by costumed dancers.

Kineticism

An art form introduced in the 1920s.

1. Optical illusion is exploited through the medium of painting in Op art.
2. Constructions seem to move along with the spectator.
3. Light strategically placed or directed can create the illusion of movement.
4. Air-powered mobiles move with the wind.
5. Mechanical parts in audiokinetic sculpture cause actual movement.

Kinetic Sculpture

It is basically designed to move or to produce optical illusion. The affirmation of Gabo (1890-1977) that "kinetic rhythm is the basic form of our perception in real time" is reflected in his transparent space sculptures. He renounced color, line, volume, and mass as superfluous to reality and espoused a time/space/movement theory.

The theory of motion in sculpture was established well before any works were produced: one of the first kinetic sculptures is attributed to Duchamp (1887-1968) when he mounted a bicycle wheel on a wood stool. It opened the way to new processes, materials, and effects in art. See Ready-Mades.

Major approaches to kinetic sculptures are energy sources such as wind, motor, magnetism, the viewer's own motion, or the spirit in which it is produced.

Kitchen Sink School (1950s)

An English school of Social Realism. Their theme was the drabness and disorder of domesticity.

Knave of Diamonds (1910-1918)

An important avant-garde and exhibition society in Russia. Besides the work of several Russian painters, they also promoted the work of Cubists, German Expressionists, and others.

Knife Work

The use of a palette knife to apply oil paint or to modify the surface of a watercolor. See Palette Knife.

Kosode

In the 9th century, T-shaped kosodes were robes worn in Japan by the common people; by the end of the 1400s, it became the principal attire for all social classes. In the late 1860s, the term "kosode" was replaced by "kimono."

These decoratively designed robes document a wealth of art styles painted, printed, dyed, or stitched, all with brilliant coloration, from the 1600s to the 1800s: architectural interiors, scenes of everyday activities, flowers, and landscapes, as well as contrasting patterns and geometric motifs, were popular.

Kouros (pl. Kouroi)

Sculptures of ideal, youthful, nude males were experiments with human figuration during the Archaic period of Greek civilization. The statues represented athletes, gods, heroes, or warriors and were placed outside of temples or at gravesites. Draped female figures were called Korai (maidens). Following Egyptian tradition, they were conventionally posed. Reflecting on the almost-divine appearance of this statuary, the poet/dramatist Sophocles wrote: "Although there are many marvels in this world, the greatest marvel of all is man."

During the Classical age, the rigid form was replaced by a more relaxed, graceful, and anatomically-correct frame. The single most rapid change in Western art is believed to have been when the Archaic style was displaced by the Classical style.

Kunsthalle (art hall)

Dating back to the 1700s and up to current times in Germany and Switzerland, the term "Kunsthalle" refers to a museum without permanent holdings of its own: a kind of counterpart to local museums. More recently, in 1993, New York Kunsthalle, a not-for-profit, European-sponsored exhibition space, was established in the Noho area of Manhattan to showcase current trends in international, contemporary art.

Kunstschutz

A special force used by Hitler during WWII (along with other similar groups), who confiscated anything of value from churches, synagogues, museums, and private homes throughout Europe and the USSR. Paintings and sculptures by Old and New Masters, tapestries, chalices, rare books and coins, antiques, and other movable property were looted; national art treasures were also expropriated. It is estimated that more than a million artworks were removed by the Nazis.

It has been recently revealed that thousands of artworks looted by the Red Army from Germany have been hidden in secret depositories, resulting in a great treasure hunt. Russian nationalists, however, now regard artworks looted by the Red Army after WWII as the legitimate spoils of victory.

A development in the recovery of looted art treasures during WWII revealed that in July, 1995 the Austrian government, after a decade of negotiation, voted to transfer ownership of nearly 8,000 artworks to the Jewish community.

L

Lacuna

A blank space or a missing part in a painting.

Landscape

A view of natural inland scenery without a story to relate. For many centuries, landscape in the Western world was used as a symbolic background. In Asian countries, however, landscape was known as a serious subject in the 3rd century A.D.

The Romans conveyed the sensations of atmosphere, light, and space in their landscapes of street scenes, architectural views, formal gardens, and mountainsides.

Altdorfer (1480-1538) is believed to be the predecessor of 17th-century landscape artists. His *Danube Landscape* is one of the first examples of a painting in the Western art world to have no human being in it at all.

Flemish artists in the 1400s/1500s are believed to have brought it to full expression, especially Patiner (1485-1525).

The Carracci family of the Bolognese School was a strong influence in the creation of pure landscape.

Van Goyen (1596-1656), Cuyp (1620-1691), van Ruisdael (1628-1682), and Hobbema (1638-1709) of the Dutch School are several of the most celebrated landscape artists.

In the 1700s/1800s the trend was to represent landscape in a romantic manner. Artists thereafter aimed at the effect of light on nature, which led to Impressionism. During the last few decades, symbolism in nature seems to have been the motif.

Several categories of landscape and the artists representative thereof are:

- Classical — Poussin (1594-1665); Claude Lorrain (1600-1682)
- Romantic — Friedrich (1774-1804); Turner (1775-1851); Constable (1776-1837); T. Rousseau (1812-1867)
- Impressionist — Sisley (1839-1899); Monet (1840-1926); Sargent (1856-1925); Lawson (1873-1939)
- Surrealist — Mirò (1893-1984); Tanguy (1900-1955)
- Expressionist — Whistler (1834-1903); Maurer (1868-1932); O'Keeffe (1887-1986)

See Hudson River School, Mindscape, and New Romantic Landscape.

Lapidary Arts

Relating to precious stones or the act of cutting them; classic are the lapidary arts that flourished in Mexico before the Conquest. Its uses were manifold: bead necklaces, pendants, ornaments for nose and ears, ceremonial masks, and the like, were exquisitely and laboriously carved.

Le Blond Ovals

Oval-shaped country scenes reproduced using the Baxter Print Process.

Liber Studiorum

A title used by Turner (1775-1851) to describe a collection of 100 drawings, etchings, and mezzotints that he assembled to show his range as a landscape artist.

Liber Veritatis

A title used by Claude Lorrain (1600-1682) to describe a collection of 200 drawings, consisting of renderings of past paintings or serving as projects for future paintings.

Lidl

A nonsense term coined by the German artist Immendorff (1945-   ) to describe a body of work: painting, sculpture, Performance art, and Happenings. The power of "art as a noise on the political stage" is demonstrated in artworks that reflect humor and the artist's commitment to the transformation of society.

Life Drawing

The drawing of a live model, usually nude and seated on a raised platform. See Academy Figure.

Life Mask

A plaster cast molded onto the face of the person being portrayed.

Light and Space (1970s)

A Southern California movement whose mediums were light, space, and kineticism. The artists were concerned with environmental issues and sensuous awareness.

Light Sculpture or Neon Art

The use of fluorescent or neon tubing, sometimes incorporating computerization, to create magical art or whimsical sculptures. New, pulsating color, kinetic light and shadow, and postmodern designs, patterns, and motifs are the elements of a new sculpture.

Limited Edition

Technically speaking, a fine art print is an original artwork in multiple edition. The artist is involved in the creation of a set number of productions of an artwork or the artisans will work under the artist's strict supervision. When the determined number of the edition has been produced, the matrix is destroyed or defaced.

A limited edition fine art print is regarded as rare and of high value because it is made with as much care and attention as a painting or sculpture. See Matrix, Signed and Numbered, and Surmoulage.

Limners (also called "face painters")

During the Middle Ages, this term applied to manuscript illuminators; in the 1500s, it applied to painters of miniature portraits. In American usage, it refers to those untrained Early American portraitists in the 1600s/1700s who lacked technical competence, but possessed a strong sense of observation and imagination. Their folk-like style had the effects of naiveté and charm.

A great number of the American limners earned their living traveling from town to town recording portraits of those who could pay for their services. They were the only artists in the Colonies; their portraits are important in terms of the history of American art.

Since the limners were mostly anonymous, they are referred to by the names of their subjects, such as the *Freake Limner* — a painting of Mrs. Freake and her child. (The limners had to mix their own paints and make their own art supplies.) See Early American Art, Folk Art, and Miniature Painting.

Limoges Boxes

Porcelain boxes traditionally made from the white clay of Limoges in France, and hand-painted by artists of that region. These tiny boxes, measuring under two inches in diameter, are regarded as expensive museum-quality pieces. They are made in a variety of whimsical, charming subjects: birdhouse, fruit, ice cream cone, grandfather clock, hat box, and so on.

Line (a mark one inch or longer)

The real or imaginary outline of any representation made by the artist according to the artist's perception. The action or quality of the line can carry the artist's meaning. A few examples are:

- Angular — Stiffness in character and manner; somber
- Bold — Strength; drama
- Curvilinear — Decorative
- Delicate — Soft, tender
- Diagonal — Movement, dynamism
- Horizontal — Calmness
- Overlapping — Illusion of forms
- Vertical — Tension; sadness

Line and Wash Drawing

An outline usually in ink that is shaded by watercolor or diluted ink. This technique was known of in antiquity and was popular during the Baroque period.

Line Drawing

The depiction of a subject according to the seemingly calligraphic quality or property of the line. Etching is regarded as a good process for the production of line drawings.

Literary Art

The subject is taken from a story: a form of illustrative or narrative art.

Little Masters

1. A title given to Greek vase painters.

2. A title applied to a group of German engravers in the 1500s, who created small, delicate plates of mythological, genre, or biblical scenes.
3. Referring to Masters of the Golden Age of Dutch Manuscript Painting.
4. Referring to Masters of the Golden Age of Dutch Painting who specialized and attained perfection in genre paintings of everyday activities: sports, leisure, peasant and bourgeois life, and moral or humorous themes.

London Group

A society of artists founded in 1913 whose purpose was to provide a comprehensive (exhibition) society for English artists who belonged to smaller groups. It was their intention to produce art in accordance with current trends in France.

Love

A rendition by Indiana (1928-   ) of the serial imagery of the word "Love" which he began in 1964. He was commissioned by the US Postal Service in 1973 to design a stamp based on that image. After 330 million stamps were sold, it became one of the most popular images created by an American artist.

Low Art

As recently defined, the popular art found in caricature, comics, graffiti, and advertising: an art form that creates iconic imagery and possesses the power to move and to excite. The critic A. Gopnik said: "Low went into high in the guise of the exotic."

Luminism

An effect obtained when light is visible through an outer layer of paint. Artists portrayed landscape realistically, but with a heavenly, glowing effect: notions of transcendence, timelessness, and tranquillity were evoked. The artists were interested in elements constituting the landscape (the hills, rivers, and lakes), rather than in what the landscape signified.

Luminists had a feeling of identification with the American scene and the beauty of light was an expression of their wonder for the natural world. Bingham (1811-1879) and Gifford (1823-1880) are recognized as leading exponents and founders of American Luminism.

Lyrical Abstraction (Abstract Lyrique)

A style characterized by a casual, informal, and psychic approach. It is expressive of a floating sensation and is usually marked by rich and lush coloration. Importance is placed on subjective and sensuous experiences.

M

Macchiaioli School (1855-1870s)

A group of painters who worked mostly in Tuscany. Landscape and narrative painting of everyday scenes and contemporary history, including battles and campaigns, were important subjects. The artists were concerned with patriotic expression, as well as artistic innovation: they wanted to create art representative of the new national consciousness.

In rendering their paintings, the artists were concerned with direct impressions — the sensation of the moment. They relied, however, on light and dark colors and ton gris (a general unifying tone) which they applied to broad, simplified areas.

Because of their genuinely novel techniques, the artists are credited with beginning the modern period of Italianate art.

Fattori (1825-1908)
DeTivoli (1826-1892)
Lega (1826-1895)
Altamura (1826-1897)
Borroni (1833-1905)

Machine-Art Performances (1990s)

A descriptive term for Performance art presented by several individual artists in California. Robots, computer- and remote-controlled sound machines, self-contained vehicles, sculptures, etc., are used to present complicated non-human spectacles. Several titles: "Performing Bodies and Smart Machines," "Walking Trees," "Mechanical Sound Orchestra," and "Bird Land." One of the best-known artists of this genre is Heckert (1957-   ). See Pseudomachines.

Macramé

The art of creative knotwork, now regarded as another expression of American Folk art, was popular as a nautical pastime in the 1800s and as a parlor art by Victorian ladies. In recent decades, it has enjoyed a comeback as a craft in the US.

Maestà (Madonna in majesty)

An altarpiece featuring the Virgin in majesty, enthroned and surrounded by angels and saints. It was a common theme in Italy during the 1200s/1300s. See Sacra Conversazione.

Magic Realism

1. The cave art of imaginary scenes drawn with the hope that a psychic union would be made between the painting and the real object.
2. Paintings characterized by a realistic style, with objects produced in minute detail.
3. The creation of mystery through strange, disturbing juxtapositions: painstaking Realism depicted in paintings characterized by a hypnotic, surrealistic atmosphere.

Mail Art or Correspondence Art

Initiated by Duchamp (1887-1968) in 1916 when he sent his ideas by postcard, it grew into a worldwide network. In addition to sending messages to other artists, a postcard conveys a drawing, a sketch, or an idea.

R. Johnson (1927-1995) revived this art form when he began to mail ephemeral material to his friends, thereby creating a small art universe. In the 1960s he founded New York Correspondence Art, a loose-knit international postal network whose members exchanged works through the mail. See Ephemera Collecting and Fluxus.

Russell (1864-1926), a painter of the American West, is known as a "word painter" because he often illustrated his correspondence with sketches in pen or watercolor.

Majolica

Originally, the term applied to Spanish tin-glazed earthenware exported from Majorca to Italy in the late Middle Ages. The term now embraces all vividly painted vessels, especially those produced in Italy from the 1400s to the 1700s, most notably those of the Renaissance.

Biblical scenes and narratives were popular, along with mythological tales and legends, which were surrounded with intricate patterns of decoritive motifs.

Mandala

See Sand Painting.

Maniera Greca (in the Greek manner)

The style used in Italianate painting of the 1100s-1200s, which was influenced by the Byzantine style: shallow space and flatness.

Manner

The "handwriting" or style of an artist. The modern usage of "in a mannered style" is regarded as disparaging.

Mannerism (1520-1580)

A term referring to a broad and diverse movement, and to a certain artistic standpoint, rather than any one style, but generally speaking the reactionary style of artists who may, perhaps, be called the first of the modern artists because they broke away from the traditional harmony and balance of Renaissance painting when they distorted or elongated the human figure and used harsh coloring and lighting: affectation of style seemed to be the motif. Social and political conditions were also influential in the development of Mannerism but, in the main, it was the result of artists working out new ideas.

Modern definitions, however, now regard Mannerism as more of an elaboration of trends set during the High Renaissance. See Baroque.

Pontormo (1494-1556)
Fiorentino (1495-1560)
Romano (1499-1546)
Parmigianino (1503-1540)
Tintoretto (1518-1594)
El Greco (1541-1614)

Manuscript Illumination

Referring to embellished handwritten texts: painted pictures, outline drawings, ornamental letters, and abstract designs, or any combination thereof.

This art form was invented by the Egyptians who illustrated Books of the Dead. It reached full expression in the Western world during the Romanesque and Gothic periods when wealthy patrons commissioned a wide variety of manuscripts such as holy scripture, fiction, treatises, and manuals. Classic is the work of Sister Diemud, of the cloister of Wessobrun, who over seven decades (from 1057 to 1130) produced 45 manuscripts "of rare beauty."

Illuminated manuscripts flourished before the age of the printing press. Every book hand-lettered and decorated, a labor of meditation and devotion, took several years to complete, and were prized as highly as gold and jewelry. See Bookworks, Illumination, and Miniature Painting.

Maquette

A small sculpture in wax or clay made as a preliminary model for the client's approval.

Marine Painting

The depiction of ship portraits, shore scenes, genre scenes of commerce or harbor activity, and yacht races.

In rendering ship portraits, the artist painted every detail accurately because the client would not tolerate anything but exact representation. In so doing, ship portraits have become important to historians, especially those representations of steamboats and sailboats by John Bard (1815-1856) and James Bard (1815-1897). See Figureheads and Seascape Painting.

Mass Art

In contrast to Folk art, it is a popular art created for an industrial society by the movies, television, newspapers, and magazines, reflecting in general the dynamics of change in fashion, style, and taste.

"Master of"

1. A term used in art history to designate the creation of anonymous works.
2. A term designating the name of a patron or the region in which the artist worked.

Masterpiece

Referring, generally, to the most important work of an artist: although a product of its time, it transcends any period in history and is universal in appeal.

Material Abstraction

Referring to the constructions of Loving (1938-   ), consisting of cut and torn paper which is lacquered, glued, and nailed together into a whirlpool of colorful interlocking planes and patterns.

Material Pictures

The technique of Nesch (1893-1975) who was influenced by German Expressionism. He created mosaic-like constructions with wire, mesh, colored glass, and nails, which were affixed to printing plates.

Matrix

Referring to the form on which the image to be printed is prepared. For example, it can be a woodblock for relief prints, a metal plate for engravings or etchings, or a smooth stone for lithographs. See Graphic Arts and Limited Edition.

Medals for Dishonor

A series of medals or small bronze reliefs created by David Smith (1906-1965) to express anti-war, anti-fascist, and anti-capitalist messages, with symbolic episodes of violence, corruption, and moral hypocrisy. Several titles: *Bombing Civilian Populations, Propaganda for War,* and *Munition Makers.* See War Art.

Media Artists

Those artists who have made radical departures from the materials and techniques used by visual artists. Theatrical events, billboards, photography, videos, films, and high tech are several avenues of expression through which artists present their works. See Post-Avant-Garde Art.

Medieval Art

Its major theme was the relationship between time and the eternal. Virtually all events, contemporary or historic, were interpreted in religious terms. See Middle Ages.

Mediterranean Art

- The Minoan Culture (c. 2600-1100 B.C.), the first civilization in Europe, was highly developed. Metalwork, including fine jewelry, small sculptures, and the decorative arts were important. Wall or fresco painting was characterized by a freer and more graceful style than found in Egypt.
- The Mycenaean Culture (1600-1100 B.C.), whose people were the first to speak Greek, excelled in metal miniatures, especially engraved seals, and carved gemstones. Jewelry, gold masks, drinking vessels, vases, and fresco painting were other avenues of expression through which they embraced the naturalistic aesthetic of the Minoans. See Greek Art.

Medium

1. The type of paint an artist uses. In a more specific sense, it refers to the vehicle or the binder for the paint being used.
2. A tool or material used by the artist.
3. The method of expression used: assemblage, the graphic arts, painting, sculpture, and so on.

Memento Mori (remember, you must die)

An object used in art as a reminder of the passing of life. In the Middle Ages, when art served mostly as a religious function, the figure of Death (usually a corpse or a skeleton in tandem with depictions of worldly enticements or pleasures) was used to inform the pious that death could be conquered and eternal life gained. Classic is the work of Holbein the Younger and Dürer of the German School.

The genesis of the *Dance of Death* (usually a sequence of genre scenes) evolved from these memento mori. The modern-day revival was precipitated by Rethel (1816-1859). More recently, German artists who survived WWI employed the theme of the *Dance of Death* to describe the corruption of war and the ills of society. See Vanitas.

Memory Painters

Referring to folk artists of the 20th century. In contrast to folk artists from centuries past, who usually created objects for daily use, memory painters most often paint scenes from their childhood. Classic is the work of "Grandma" Moses (1860-1961).

Mesopotamia (3500-1000 B.C.)

This culture is known for its royal graves, highly decorative architecture, and statuary in the service of the gods. Kings often commissioned monuments to commemorate victories in war or royal hunts. In later years, these monuments developed into picture-chronicles. They excelled in narrative relief, metalwork, and the carving of gemstones and bronzes. (As a note to history, the arts of Mesopotamia and of the Aegean world vanished almost entirely from human sight and memory until very nearly our own times.)

Mesopotamia, like Egypt, was a leading cultural center of the ancient world before the rise of Greece.

Metaphysical Painting (Pittura Metafisica) (1915-1920)

A school founded by Carra (1881-1966), de Chirico (1888-1978), Morandi (1890-1964), and DePisis (1896-1956) in Italy. They painted surrealistic pictures expressive of a strange, nightmarish world. The result is an uneasy assemblage of images in a peculiarly silent world.

Mezzotint Prototypes (an English tone process of engraving)

It was a common practice for artists to paint only the face from life and to copy the body from prototypes. Patroon painters had collections of them so their patrons could choose the desired pose and costume.

Micro Galleries

Major museums have recently opened sophisticated multimedia systems that guide visitors through virtual tours of their permanent collections. On-line surfers on the World Wide Web can also obtain museum information and a guide to exhibitions.

World-famous auction houses offer learning tools for auction neophytes and in-depth materials for connoisseurs on the Web site. Users can also read about auctions, obtain knowledge about the arts, collecting, and appraisal, as well as travel through Auction Adventures.

This new technology, if used to its fullest potential, offers museums without walls and exhibitions without end.

Middle Ages (500s-1500s)

A term first used to describe the medieval period when religion was the dominating force in life and art. The early Middle Ages represent the first age of Europe when the culture of the modern world was formulated with the establishment of universities, political institutions, national identity, and the growth of Catholic Christendom.

Arts and crafts endemic to these centuries consisted primarily of fresco painting, illuminated manuscripts, relief sculpture, tapestries, and stained glass, all representative of aesthetic and religious values.

Middle Distance

A term used in landscape painting to define a level surface behind the foreground.

Mindscape

A term coined by Wright (1948-   ) for his painted landscapes. His premise is that when one reads poetry repeatedly, it becomes a part of one's inner self. This theory is applied to his artworks when he translates his own perception of the spiritual or psychological essence of nature, as well as its beauty, onto a surface without actually copying from nature.

Miniature Painting

A term used to describe several styles of small-scale painting, measuring from less than one inch to about 15 inches high, with fine, exquisite brushwork as a distinguishing characteristic:

1. Illuminated manuscripts.
2. Portraits/medallions by specialists in England from the 1500s to the 1800s. They were known as "paintings in little." Female artists excelled. During Renaissance years, portrait medallions were regarded as a perfect vehicle for the sitter's aspirations to immortality: religious leaders, the aristocracy, and wealthy merchants all had their images captured.
3. In America, from about 1740 to 1839 (when photographic portraiture began), miniature painting was a flourishing art form and practiced by many well-known portraitists. These portraits were intended as "affectionate mementos." In sum, miniature painting was an important aspect of 18th- and 19th-century American art.
4. Today's miniaturists work with a broader range of subjects, painting landscapes, religious and historic scenes, as well as portraiture.

Minimal Art or Minimalism (1960s-1970s)

An art form that is neither illusionistic nor allusive. Basically, the reduction of art to its essentials: a purified, simple, geometric, and sculptural art form. Its emphasis is on the inner nature of objects, and the viewer must perceive and respond to that inner nature; it is this experience that is the motif. The artist Morris (1931-   ) said:

"Simplicity of shape does not necessarily equate with simplicity of experience."

Minimalist painters have rendered large fields of monochromes. Classic is the work of Reinhardt (1913-1967) who created hard-edged, severely minimal abstract works. He believed in reducing art to its purest spiritual form. See Hard-Edge Painting and Primary Structures.

Minjung Art (people's art)

A contemporary movement in South Korea with its beginnings in the early 1970s; it was a reaction to modern-art styles. Thereafter, the major source of commonality between artists was the commitment to achieving a democratic society. (Under former military regimes, radical artists had been jailed and their artworks destroyed.) As society has moved toward democracy, the most important cause now for all Minjung artists is unification of South and North Korea.

Minor Arts

A special group that involves the use of solid materials, such as textiles, glass, wood, and metal, to produce items that are useful, decorative and, for the most part, possess qualities of beauty and aesthetic pleasure.

Mirror Painting

A technique practiced by Pistoletto (1933-   ) when he traced a series of life-size photographs in arrested movement onto transparent paper and then cut out and pasted them onto sheets of polished steel which were painted in sombre colors. The steel sheets were then arranged to reflect the image of the viewer.

Mitate

A Japanese term referring to imitation — a scene from history or legend is imitated, but brought up to date with complete disregard for time, costume, and sexual gender. Such parodies were common in Ukiyo-e artworks.

Mixed Media

Artworks produced in more than one kind of medium.

Mobile

A term describing the hanging sculptures of Calder (1898-1976), which he began to create in the 1930s. They were made of metal rods, wire, glass, and plastic and arranged in inventive forms. Calder wanted to balance the movement of colored form with air current, giving the effect of airborne sculptures. He said: "When everything goes right, a mobile is a piece of poetry that dances with the joy of life and surprises."

Calder developed a new form of expression in Modern art; his work constituted a major breakthrough in sculptural form. See Kineticism, Kinetic Sculpture, and Stabile.

Modello or Modelletto

When a painting was commissioned during centuries past, the artist would often make a small version of it for the patron's approval.

Modern Art

Throughout its history, Modern art has initiated dozens of styles. A common theme is the artist's desire to simplify and to get down to basics. In each of its movements, the style most often reflects a reaction to an earlier style. Basically, Modern art's major approaches are (1) self-expression and experimentation and (2) desire for harmony through a systematic but intuitive arrangement. Matisse's (1869-1954) statement that "exactitude is not truth" seems to embody the thesis of Modern art.

Several pioneers of Modern art:

- Manet (1832-1883) He was regarded as a revolutionary because he painted life as it appeared to his senses, without using conventional methods. Manet applied bold, contrasting colors side by side. He was closely allied with the Impressionists and has been called "a painter's painter."
- Cézanne (1839-1906) He is known as the father of Modern art because he used shape and value to reinforce the effects of his colors, enabling him to evoke the sensation of depth. See 20th Century Art.
- Gauguin (1848-1903) He used large areas of flat color. His figures and landscapes transcend reality and symbolize spiritual and universal themes.
- Van Gogh (1853-1890) He made known his inner feelings with expressive, pulsating brushwork and brilliant, radiant, and decorative color. Color was his language. His work was influential in the formation of Expressionism.
- Munch (1863-1944) The first modern painter to study the personality. He was concerned with humanity, inner visions, and dreams.
- Stieglitz (1864-1946) His foresight led to tireless advocacy of the modernist movement. See 291 Group.
- Kandinsky (1866-1944) and Klee (1879-1940) Their discoveries, innovations, and writings were influential in the development of Modern art. Klee's summation of its purpose was "not to reflect the visible, but to make visible."
- Léger (1881-1955) The machine was a great influence on his work. He was one of the first artists whose paintings focused on modern urban life with the portrayal of solid, machine-like structures in flat colors with dark outlines. He thought "beauty is everywhere."
- Picasso (1881-1973) The master of the modern School of Paris, whose range of skills from painting to theatre design gives his genius the same place in the 20th century as Giotto in the Middle Ages and Michelangelo during the Renaissance.
- Pach (1883-1958) As artist, critic, lecturer, and art historian, he was a catalyst and spokesperson for the modernist movement in the US and played a major role in organizing exhibitions, most notably the Armory Show.
- Davis (1894-1964) He was an articulate and effective spokesperson for modernism in the US. It was his belief that Modern art was the most appropriate art for present-day America. Davis was probably the most important American artist to explore Cubism.

Modernism

1. The theory of Modern art rejecting past styles. In the early 1900s, architects, sculptors, painters, and designers all sought change and innovation that reflected the modern world. The machine became an important symbol.

2. Art historian F. Karl defined it in terms of innovative color systems, fresh arrangements and utilizations of the picture surface, new geometries, awareness of planes, and dynamism of line, shape, and mass.

As a note to history, the term "modern" was first used in the late 1500s to distinguish that period from centuries past.

Monolith

A single but huge stonepiece shaped into sculptural form, such as an obelisk or a column. See Stela.

Montage

A composite picture resulting from the placing of materials, prints, or photographs in a preconceived design to produce comical, convulsive, or lyrical fantasies. See Photomontage.

Monte Sainte-Victoire

Cézanne (1839-1906) rendered 80 oil and watercolor studies of this mountain landscape. The mountain was always new to him in every season, every light, and every mood.

Morellian Principles

These were formulated to study the minute details of a painting to reveal the "handwriting" of the artist, a method used to detect counterfeit work.

Mosaic

A method of decoration using small pieces of colored glass, stone, or ceramic which are inlaid on a background, usually a wall, to create a design or a picture: form and color are part of a careful program.

Mosaic designs or compositions were an integral part of the architectural effect during centuries past. This craft was known in Mesopotamia, Egypt, Greece, Islam, and Christendom, but its use in making large pictorial compositions appears to have been born in Greece and developed in Rome. The mosaic work found in the churches of Ravenna and Venice is classic.

In the contemporary age, Pueblo Indians in New Mexico create turquoise plaques. More recently, in 1992, *Gorgeous Mosaic*, representing a view of skyscrapers, was installed as a floor design in a Manhattan skyscraper. It contains 150,000 stones.

In 1995, the city of Rome commissioned artists from all over the world to design mosaics for metro stations. The designs were transferred by a special computer to glass-paste tiles.

Well-made mosaic is the most durable of all decorative techniques. See Pattern and Decoration.

Motion

The creation of movement in artworks includes the following dynamics:

1. Arrested or inactive, usually seen in two-dimensional painting.
2. Free, whereby movement is liberated by the deep space of perspective.

3. The stroboscopic effect of successive stages in a single image or the afterimage of a moving object produced by blurring, streaking, etc.
4. A change in measurable quality such as size, hue, and brightness.
5. Eye-movement

Mount

1. To arrange or assemble for display.
2. The material on which a picture is placed.

Mourning Pictures

From the death of George Washington in 1799 until the 1820s, this American Folk art, regarded as a "ladies art form," was popular in producing the iconography of mourning: paintings, needlework, carvings on furniture, and weavings were the usual mediums used to depict graveyards, gravestones, monuments, and mourners.

Mujeres Muralistas, Las (1973-1976)

The first women's mural collective, born in San Francisco. The artists produced public murals fusing the tradition of Mexican muralists with contemporary history. These murals covey the principal message of ethnic pride and self-determination of the Latin people. See Chicano Art.

Multimedia

In terms of the audio/visual world, it includes a combination of sight and sound, usually controlled by a computer. Some or all of the following media are employed to present artworks: animation, audio, film, graphics, still images, text, and video.

Multiples

A term used to describe graphic arts and cast sculptures that are produced in unlimited numbers.

Mural

The art form of painting large or monumental pictures on walls and ceilings can be traced to early cultures of millenniums past. In more recent centuries, particularly during the Middle Ages, this medium, in the form of fresco painting, reached full expression in the Western world.

In the US, during the 1800s, many murals were made for public buildings. Hunt (1824-1879) painted sections of the State Capitol of New York; LaFarge (1835-1910) was responsible for the monumental interior of Trinity Church in Boston.

The work of Mexican artists Orozco (1883-1949), Rivera (1886-1957), and Siqueiros (1896-1974) is classic of mural work in the modern age. See Revolutionary Art and Tres Grandes.

During the Great Depression of the 1930s in the US, numerous murals were created for public buildings/projects under the direction of the Public Buildings Administration. See WPA.

The 27 mural panels rendered by Refregier (1905-1979) in a San Francisco post office constitute one of the largest projects executed for the federal government: historic events occurring in California, including strikes, persecutions, and miscarriages of justice, are illustrated. When the House UnAmerican Activities Committee tried to have these murals destroyed in 1953, it did not succeed.

More recently, however, this medium has become a popular form of expression in inner-city neighborhoods. The murals focus on the lives, problems, and culture of the people. Frequently, artists are urged to create murals only after they have determined the subject, design, and production in collaboration with residents. In essence, the murals are billboards that tell a community's story. See Public Art.

In 1976, Baca (1946-   ) and dozens of assistants, including teenagers, began to create the Great Wall Project in the San Fernando Valley. As the largest mural in the world, it depicts the history of California, from pre-Columbian years to current times, and includes images of many historical figures. See Fresco, Mujeres Muralistas, and Wall Painting.

Museum

An institution dedicated to the collection, care, study, and display of artworks, crafts, history, science, technology, and regional artifacts as objects of lasting value or interest.

The Akadamie der Bildenden Künste in Vienna recently celebrated its 300th anniversary. The British Museum opened its doors to the public in 1759. Another early museum was the Louvre: although it had its cultural beginnings in the 14th century, the museum itself was inaugurated in 1793 when the royal palace and all its treasures became state property. It was referred to as a "people's art museum."

The term "museum" seems to have first appeared in the US in 1773 when the Charleston Library Society in South Carolina voted to annex a museum; it had a mixture of art and science exhibits.

Peale's Museum in Philadelphia, established in 1802, played an important role in the museological growth of the US. Portraits by Peale (1741-1827) of Revolutionary War heroes were hung next to objects of science and natural history; ethnography was represented by figures of Native Americans and their utensils and weapons; models of machines were also displayed.

This country's first three major art museums in Boston, Washington, D.C., and New York City were all incorporated in 1870. They were the Boston Museum of Fine Arts, The Corcoran Gallery, and the Metropolitan Museum of Art, respectively. Between the two world wars, 300 new art museums were established in the US.

In recent decades, art museums have undertaken a number of new activities such as installing restaurants and cafes, giving guided tours, concerts, and lectures, showing films, selling articles related to art (books, posters, games, jewelry, and objets d'art) and, most important, providing education facilities for children.

The world's great museums include: The National Gallery in London, The Louvre in Paris, Alte Pinakothek in Munich, Kunsthistorisches in Vienna, The Prado in Madrid, The Uffizi in Florence, The National Museum in Tokyo, The Metropolitan in New York City, and The Smithsonian in Washington, D.C. See Hermitage and Micro Galleries.

Museum of Modern Mythology

This museum, founded in 1982 in San Francisco to display the trademarks, logos, and other images that have become icons of American culture through advertising, contains a permanent collection of more than 3,000 items such as models of the Michelin Tire Man, Mister Clean, and Charlie the Tuna.

Mythic Art

In recent times, an attempt to have a dialog with the immaterial world, especially as in Ethnographic art; in particular, the recent artistic creations of Native Americans. These artists have created paintings, collages, wood carvings, constructions, assemblages, and other artworks, using motifs that strongly identify their ethnicity, political or philosophical beliefs, concern for the environment, and their attitude toward white America's desecration of the land and destruction of the property rights of their people.

Mythological Painting (1400s-1800s)

The painting of stories or allegorical narrative involving supernatural elements or ancient tales. The paintings of Titian (1490-1576), called "Poesie" (poetries), taken largely from Ovid, are classic of the mythological theme. Poussin (1594-1665) found in mythology many artistic subjects: classic is *Blind Orion Searching for the Rising Sun.*

N

Nabis, les (the Prophets) (1889-1899)

A group of artists who possessed diverse talents. Although their paintings were of cabaret scenes, expressionistic landscapes, and views of city and country life, central to their philosophy was the desire to communicate meaning through color and line. Symbolism was the principal motif.

The artists were active in the fields of applied art, decorative arts, graphic arts, painting, and theatre. They left their mark everywhere: in the home they designed wallpaper, textiles, tapestries, furniture, and painted plates; in the theatre they designed decors, costumes, and programs; in the graphic arts they produced posters, drawings, and lithographs.

Sérusier (1863-1927)
Ranson (1864-1909)
Vallotton (1865-1925)
Ibels (1867-1936)
Roussel (1867-1944)
Bonnard (1867-1947)
Vuillard (1868-1940)

See Intimist Painters.

Naive Art (sometimes called Primitive Art)

An art marked by lack of perspective (flat space), directness of vision, simplicity, humor, innocence, and naturalism; at times, somewhat similar to cartoon imagery.

The Naive artist presents a combination of realistic objects and imaginary or dream-like objects painted in minute detail, but often without the technical skills necessary to produce accuracy: the artist is usually self-taught.

H. Rousseau (1844-1910)
Kane (1860-1934)
"Grandma" Moses (1860-1961)
Bombois (1883-1970)
Pippin (1888-1946)

Narrative Art

The relating of a story in a series of events or in a decisive moment.

From Early Christian years through the Renaissance, the sacred story was the major narrative theme: manuscript illumination, altarpieces, fresco cycles, and stained-glass windows were the vehicles for illustrating the Christian story in terms of key events.

One of the most remarkable narrative renditions is that of *The Battle of Alexander and Darius* by Altdorfer (1480-1538).

Steen (1626-1679), acting as a moralist and storyteller, created pictures of family life such as *The Way You Hear It Is the Way You Sing It*. Hogarth (1697-1764) and Greuze (1725-1805) are known for their morality themes. Krimmel (1787-1821) painted hundreds of humorous or eventful scenes of American life.

In the US, during the 1800s, narrative paintings were a popular form of education and entertainment. See National Paintings.

In Modern art, narrative uses simple imagery to act out a story.

National Paintings

Bingham (1811-1879) rendered regional and genre portrayals of American scenes that seem to come to life in paintings titled *Fur Traders Descending the Missouri, The County Election, The Jolly Flatboatmen*, and so on. These paintings of fur traders drifting downriver, raftsmen playing cards, racing steamboats, and shooting matches were regarded as "truly American" and were meant to be "read," as paintings of this kind were meant to be, in the mid-1800s.

National Work

A term coined by Trumbull (1756-1843) to describe his series of portraits of American generals and prominent political figures. His historical paintings, reproduced in countless illustrations, have become part of the American tradition. The artist is known as the father of grand-style painting in the US.

Naturalism

1. A representation giving the effect of accuracy without creating the illusion of reality, as rendered in Naive or Primitive art.
2. The interpretation of some ideal or imaginary subject; in contrast to Realism, the artist is concerned with what is current.
3. Differences between Naturalism and Realism were distinguished by art historian Canaday as follows: Moral ideas are incorporated into Realism and painters paint what they see in the hope of finding fundamental truths in commonplace objects; whereas, Naturalism incorporates the spectacles of life such as vice and ugliness, beauty and sweetness, the ephemeral, the moment of life.

See Visual Realism.

Nazarenes (early 1800s)

A group of Austrian and German painters who were inspired by the work of Italian fresco painters of the Early Renaissance. Art, in their opinion, was a religious mission. They sought a romantic purity to revitalize the "soul" of the German state. Their work was produced in a flat, archaic style, using light tones.

Neo-Abstraction (1980s-1990s)

The nonrepresentational, independent work of artists who have a wide range of attitudes toward art. They seem to have re-invented the language of abstraction.

Neo-Avant-Garde Art

An art form that is in continual growth.

Neoclassicism (1770-1830)

The deliberate return to antiquity, as manifested in the disciplines of architecture, sculpture, painting, and the decorative arts.

Artists reacted to the frivolity of ornate Baroque-Rococo by reworking scenes from antiquity and creating ideological scenes of the Napoleonic Empire, marked by inflexible laws of composition and clearly defined ideal forms. David (1748-1825), a leading exponent of the Classical tradition, insisted the subject have grandeur and a moral: his *Death of Socrates* became a manifesto of this style.

Gérard (1770-1837)	Guerin (1774-1833)
Gros (1771-1835)	Ingres (1780-1867)

See Romanticism.

Neo-Expressionism (sometimes called Neo-Figuration) (1980s)

A generic term for postmodern art that began and developed in Germany. Angst-ridden emotionalism and freely expressive brushwork are emphasized. Stimulating imagery and figural representations are appropriated from older, non-traditional art and the media.

Neo-Geo (1980s)

Two of its approaches: Geometric Abstraction and a mixed media. It has been referred to by several names, but Halley (1953-), one of its exponents, prefers "Simulationism" because natural things have been replaced by technical methods: movies in place of life, bio-mechanical control of life, and so on.

The only source of commonality between the artists is the depiction of imagery rather than original sources; they feel the world totally consists of imagery.

Neo-Iconography

The Taiwanese-born artist Chen (1936-) has adopted this term for his art: a kind of artistic whimsy in which recognizable historical or cultural images are appropriated and combined with newly made portraits and scenarios that transcend time and space, East and West, past and present. Titles of paintings include *Post-Van Gogh Series, East & West Series, Venus Series*, and *The Spirit of Liberty*. See Chinoise Pop.

Neo-Impressionism (also called Pointillism or Divisionism) (late 1800s)

A term coined by the French critic Fénéon in 1886 when he viewed artworks rendered in the Pointillist technique. In a struggle to make their canvases brighter than those of the Impressionists, Seurat (1859-1891) and Signac (1863-1935) turned to scientific color theory to create true light brilliance. Paint was applied methodically in points of color in close proximity: the colors fuse in the viewer's eye from a distance. See Optical Mixture.

Seurat cared mostly about color and pattern; his purpose in painting was to bring about "an act of harmony." See Post-Impressionism.

Neo-Plasticism

The style of the De Stijl movement which expressed a desire for complete objectivity. Mondrian (1872-1944) created its motif: simplicity and no illusion. He wanted to portray the harmony of the universe by using vertical and horizontal lines in rectangles that were painted in primary colors only, with accents of black, white, and gray. Neo-Plasticism had a far-reaching influence in the development of a modern aesthetic theory.

Neo-Primitivism (early 1900s)

A Russian form of expression. The artists used as their sources signboard painting, peasant wood carving, and children's art in their portrayals of rudimentary, naive scenes that reflect a barbaric vigor.

Neo-Realism (1913-1914)

A philosophy developed by English artists Gilman (1876-1919), Gore (1878-1914), and Ginner (1878-1952). They thought Realism should be created on canvas in accordance with the artist's interpretation of nature, a belief similar to that of the Impressionists.

Neo-Romanticism (late 1920s-1930s)

A movement whose themes of sadness, mystery, and fantasy seem to represent a sort of psychological escapism. Many of the works reveal nostalgia for the past, estrangement, or loss in the depiction of melancholy figures, ruined landscapes, and empty cities.

New Artists' Association (Neue Kunstlervereinigung or NKV)

A movement formed in Munich in 1909 by a group of Expressionists who reacted against Realism. The artists wanted to experiment, without restriction, with the inner world and with impressions received from nature. A search was made for nothing but the essentials. It gradually became a force for all modern European artists.

New English Art Club (1886-1916)

This association was founded by artists whose paintings were representative of contemporary, progressive art. Naturalistic painting was their motif; they wanted to follow "the methods long practiced in France — vivid and simple studies of nature."

New Figuration (sometimes called New Realism)

An art form somewhere between abstraction and figuration in which the artist attempts to communicate the drama of contemporary man. In so doing, the image may take on a grotesque or burlesque appearance: a kind of black humor that often reflects the isolation and terror of the modern human condition. The English artist Bacon (1909-1992) is well known for this technique.

New Hope School (1887-1930s)

Lathrop (1859-1938) was the founder of this Bucks County group near the Delaware River in Pennsylvania; Redfield (1869-1965) was the acknowledged leader. These countryside painters used techniques of Impressionism in their representations of everyday life, landscapes, and village and port scenes. See American Impressionism.

New Image Painting and Sculpture (1970s)

A new label for a loosely connected group of artists who used simplified figuration in large, abstract fields. Their primary interest was to renew the art of painting, with imagery as a motif. The new images created were often flat figural outlines set against deep or monochromatic colors that were painted or constructed with eccentric or whimsical touches.

New Objectivity, the (die Neue Sachlichkeit) (1920s-early 1930s)

Social outrage was the theme. The artists used harsh verism to portray current social evils. Their work was satirical, cynical, and emotional. Classic is the work of Dix (1891-1969) and Grosz (1893-1959). See Verism and War Art.

New Romantic Landscape

The return to landscape painting may have been an indication of artistic reaction to the recent focus on man-made objects and imagery. In its new format, however, the conventions of representation are no longer used to depict the environment but, instead, fragmented landscapes are expressed in inventive abstractions. No sense of the rational seems to exist because of the highly unique concepts of landscape and the materials used.

Many of the artists live in the city and get their ideas for landscapes from photographs, ads, or posters: they see nature through images and are separated from it. A good number of the artworks reflect on the precarious state of the environment.

New World Surrealism (1930s-1940s)

Although the techniques of Surrealism are the same, the Latin American contribution to this genre is significant: mystical, fantastical, and magical phenomena are integrated into everyday life. Classic is the work of Lam (1902-1982) and Varo (1908-1963). See Auto-Iconography.

New York School

See Abstract Expressionism.

Ningyo

For centuries, Japanese dolls have served as sculptures, magic charms, learning tools, souvenirs, and gifts. The most elaborately dressed dolls depict warriors or royalty. Occasionally, the dolls were presented in tableaux such as musicians performing on miniature instruments or in tea ceremonies.

Noirs

A term coined by Redon (1840-1916) for artworks created over a period of 20 years when he worked almost exclusively in black and white, producing hundreds of charcoal drawings and lithographs containing mysterious and melancholy images. See Symbolism.

Nonfigurative Art, Nonobjective Art, Nonrepresentational Art

Generally, the arrangement of forms and colors not intended to represent an actual object or any element in nature. Specifically, in nonobjective art, forms, lines, colors, and textures are manipulated for their own sake. See Abstract Art.

North American Indian and Eskimo Art

Generally speaking, for a period of over 5,000 years, the artistic productions of native cultures, from the Arctic Circle to Tierra del Fuego, range from beautifully made objects of everyday life to expressions of deep spirituality and works of fine art.

The making of crafts was an integral part of Indian life. Technical proficiency and productivity were the criteria for prestige rather than originality in color and design. Form usually followed function. Gradually, however, decorative elements developed in the production of such articles as moccasins, blankets, and clothing, with symbols of prestige, religion, or mythology.

Painting was important for the decoration of pottery and clothing. Sand painting, connected to healing, was practiced by the Navajo tribe. Well-known Indian crafts include basket-weaving, embroidery, featherworks, leatherworks, the making of silver and turquoise jewelry, woven articles, masks, rock painting, kachina dolls, ceremonial artifacts, textiles, pottery, wood carving, and the use of beads as decorative items.

Native American art has never been static; artists have always embraced new ideas, cultural symbols, and materials. Because of diverse cultures, artistic creations have varied such as the Hopis in the Southwest, known for kachina dolls, and the Northwest Coast Indians, known for totem poles depicting stories and traditions.

Eskimo arts and crafts were closely related to the struggle for survival. They are represented by small ivory sculptures, harpoon-weights, masks, and utilitarian objects. The craft of sculpted artifacts increased in popularity so that in recent centuries they became objects sold as souvenirs. More recently, soapstone has become a popular medium for small sculptures.

As in Indian culture, Inuit art depended on the materials available and, in those areas where wood was available, wood carving became a major craft.

In the modern world, Native Americans have adopted the art forms of painting, drawing, and printmaking, and have renewed the crafts of carving and costume-making for traditional reasons and for commercial purposes. See Blackware, Haida Art, Mythic Art, Parfleche, Petroglyph, and Primitive Art.

Northern European Art (sometimes called the Northern Renaissance)

Some of its highlights:

In Flemish art, during the 1400s, a great change occurred. With the exceptional depiction of Realism, artists became perfect eyewitnesses to history. *The Betrothal of Arnolfini* by Jan van Eyck is classic of this manifestation; this painting is regarded as a landmark in the history of painting. The technical contributions of the brothers van Eyck, including the perfection of oil painting, were a direct cause of the revolution of painting.

In the 1600s, the Netherlands produced the major painters of Northern Europe. From 1600 to 1675 there were more than twice as many master painters as there were in all the rest of Europe combined.

In German art, during the 1400s, the invention of the graphic arts launched an economical method for supplying the populace with woodcuts, playing cards, and book-blocks. The mastery of technical problems was seen in the work of several artists of the German School. In the 1500s, painting was perfected to a high degree with the work of Altdorfer, Baldung-Grien, Dürer, and Grünewald.

In French art, during the 1400s, the development of a distinctly French style was reflected in portraiture and in manuscript illumination. In the 1500s, the beginnings of the Renaissance could be seen in a courtly style after Francis I had commissioned Italian artists. A Franco-Italianate style developed in architecture.

North Light

The exposure most favored by artists because of its stability.

Nouveaux Réalistes (1959-1964)

A group of artists, led by the French critic Pierre Restany, who promoted a philosophy of "sociological reality." (The theme seemed to be the reduction of an argument to an absurdity.) Nouveau Réalisme was defined as "new perceptual approaches to the real" in a signed statement by the artists. Their works of "collective singularity" have been divided into various categories, most notably assemblage, action-spectacles, décollage, and painting. See Cosmogenies, Décollage, Junk Art and Sculpture, and Transitory Artworks.

Novecento Italiano (Italian Twentieth Century) (1922-1943)

A movement that rejected avant-garde art. The artists wanted to return to classical composition and to revive large figurative paintings based on Renaissance tradition. They also shared Futurism's strong nationalist impulse.

November Group, the (die Novembergruppe)

A movement formed in Berlin in 1918 by Klein (1876-1954) and Pechstein (1881-1955). They were concerned with reconstruction and the fine arts; it was their hope to bring about a close relation between artists and the public. The movement became too large and split into two segments: one that wanted to participate in the social struggle through Realism, which led to the formation of the New Objectivity; the second group wanted to participate in the exploration of the soul, which eventually led to Surrealism.

Nude Descending a Staircase

This portrait by Duchamp (1887-1968), one of the first examples of Modern art seen in the US, created a furor at the Armory Show in 1913. It was executed in multiple images with the intention of portraying movement; it was Duchamp's personal version of Cubism.

Nude Portraiture

Many interpretations are given to this term. In the Greek classical era, sculptors idealized the human form so much that their creations in perfect proportions seemed almost divine. See Kouros.

During medieval years, Christian theology defined four symbolic types: the natural state of man; spiritual suffering/poverty; innocence/truth; lust/vanity.

During Early Renaissance years, the nude, whether painted or carved, re-emerged as an expression of ideal beauty; once again, as in Greek and Roman culture, human figures seemed to be immortalized.

Although the female nude is highly visible in Western culture, until the late 1800s/

early 1900s the male nude was the main subject of academic study. In Modern art, the nude is portrayed according to the style of expression practiced by many 20th-century artists, namely, Bonnard, Freud, Matisse, Modigliani, Pearlstein, Ramos, Renoir, and Wesselmann.

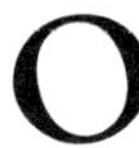

Objective Painting

An attempt to reconstruct the world as seen in its reality, in contrast to abstract or nonobjective painting. See Realism.

Objet d'Art

An object of some artistic worth, usually a decorative curio such as metalwork or ceramicware.

Objet de Fantaisie

Classic are over 150,000 objects created by the House of Fabergé. These objects are marked by their wit, ingenuity of design, and extravagance. Easter eggs are probably the most splendid and well known of these exquisitely created works, along with cigarette cases, cane handles, and snuffboxes, all adorned with gold, silver, diamonds, rubies, or sapphires.

Objet de Vertu

An object of value because of its workmanship, usually a small precious ornament such as a vase, jewelry, or statuette.

Oceanic Art

Art of the South Pacific: an area from New Guinea across the South Pacific Ocean to Easter Island, north to Hawaii and south to New Zealand. It refers especially to Ethnographic art.

As in other prehistoric civilizations, only a vague picture remains of the development of Oceanic ethnology. In general, Polynesian artists excelled in carving wood, ivory, and stone figural sculptures in sizes ranging from tiny to gigantic. Tattooing was regarded as a prestigious art form. In Melanesia, intricate wood carvings, representing human figuration, were set in tableaux associated with dramatic rituals. Cult sculptures and paintings have been found on walls of buildings, such as the Men's Houses, in New Guinea. See Aboriginal Art and Primitive Art.

Ocean Park

A series of abstract, architectural landscapes of the Ocean Park section of Santa Monica that Diebenkorn (1922-1993) had rendered from 1967 to recent years. They are regarded as his trademark and are included in almost every important contemporary collection.

Odalisque

A partially clothed or nude female figure painted in an Oriental setting.

Oeuvre

A French term referring to the lifework of an artist.

Oil Paint

A pigment is mixed with a drying agent and an oil. Although its history is not definite, it was known of in ancient times for tinting and varnishing and was used primarily for practical items. Medieval painters used it as a preservative and for painting on metal and stone surfaces. In the 1300s/1400s, Italian painters restricted its use to detail. (It was also used to paint sculptures and to glaze over tempera paintings.)

Perfected by Flemish artists, it enabled painters to capture detail more realistically and to obtain unheard-of effects of light and color. The Venetians were the first to use layer after layer of oil paint on stretched canvas, rather than on wooden panels. See Northern European Art.

Old Master

1. A term used to describe master painters from centuries past, particularly during the Renaissance and Baroque periods.
2. A distinguished artist/craftsperson from the years before the early 1800s.

Oleograph

A print resembling an oil painting.

"One-Shot" Painting

In the 1950s/1960s, Louis (1912-1962) began to pour thinned acrylic in smooth streams down the surface of unprimed canvas. If a mistake occurred, the failed painting would be discarded. Louis inspired others to experiment with acrylics and colors. See *Veils.*

Op Art (1960-1970s)

Its basic premise is that the eye can be tricked because of optical illusion when color contrasts are juxtaposed: a kind of dynamism that depends on visual devices. Basically, Op art is based on pattern perception; the sense of it can only be completed by the viewer.

One technique creates afterimages or an illusion through intense color and geometric pattern; another technique uses the effects of light and shade. Whatever technique, an effect on the retina results, sometimes to the detriment of the viewer. Vasarely (1908-1997) is recognized as the father of Op.

Open Edition

See Multiples.

Opening

A private showing of an exhibition, usually a day or two prior to opening for the public. Museums may have openings that extend to a week or more for its members and guests.

Opens

A series of paintings by Motherwell (1915-1991), who based his imagery derivative, in part, of "beautifully proportioned" doors and windows of Mexican adobe houses. The artist was inspired to paint rectangular shapes in fields of color when he leaned a small painting against a larger painted surface, resulting in one rectangle superimposed on another.

Optical Mixture

A color theory involving the analysis of light and color and their interaction, a laborious and time-consuming process. Colors in tiny points and dots (the splitting of color) are applied to the canvas; these fuse in the viewer's eye from a distance. See Neo-Impressionism.

Opus Anglicanum (English work)

One of the most famous products of medieval England was its extraordinary needlework.

Oriental/Asian Art

Its common art objects: handscrolls, hanging scrolls, folding fans, albums, and screens. See Chinese Art and Japanese Art.

Origami

The intricate art of paper folding, with its roots in China, is now a popular art form in Japan and the US. It entails folding paper into two- or three-dimensional objects in varied geometric, abstract, fantastical, or realistic forms. Experts can create a simple piece in a minute; elaborate pieces can take hours.

Orphism or Orphic Cubism (1909-1914)

A term coined by the critic Apollinaire to define a development of Cubism: the art of painting new, abstract, geometric forms, basically non-existent structures. Color was the primary concern: the effects of recession, space, and movement were sought through the use of simultaneous contrast and the interplay of color.

The artists saw the world as a composition of dynamic forces which led them to paint abstractions of line and color. See Rayonism and Vorticism.

Ottonian Renaissance (A.D. 919-1060)

This revival took place in Germany under the Ottos and the Henrys. It was marked by exceptional manuscript illumination executed in a lively and expressive manner. The highest attainment of Ottonian art is the series of visions from both Old and New Testaments, represented with an explosive power never seen before in figurative art. Fresco painting was also important. Work in wood, ivory, gold, and silver was outstanding. See Romanesque.

Outsider Art

A term recently adopted to refer to artworks created by mental patients, recluses, and spiritualists who are driven by some inner need or an imaginary or fanciful vision or dream. In the US, "outsider" has become a catchphrase in the media, used in place of other terms such as art brut, intuitive, naive, self-taught, or visionary. Major themes include religion, family, contemporary culture, memory, and fantasy.

Classic is the work of Wölfli (1864-1930), a long-time inmate of a mental asylum, who created thousands of artworks, including 45 text-and picture-filled books containing 25,000 pages, 1,600 illustrations, and 1,500 collages. His works have sold for many thousands of dollars.

P

Painted Tintype

Referring to a photograph on a thin sheet of iron, a low-cost technique which became popular around 1860. The range of overpainting varied from a mere touch of color to painting the entire picture. These tintypes were the cheapest type of photography: when they were framed, any family could afford to have a "painting" hung on the wall.

Painterly

1. The definition of form by the merging of color and tone, light and shade.
2. Painting in which all elements are in accordance with technical/aesthetic standards.

Painting

The use by artists of different mediums, usually on a flat surface, to create an image according to the artist's conception or perception. Prior to medieval years, painting was an everyday task or a necessary vocation. Until the 1400s, walls, pottery, books, and furniture were the main objects of painting. See Fine Arts.

Leonardo da Vinci expressed the view that "painting is poetry that can be seen."

Palette

1. The complete set of colors for use in the medium of painting.
2. A tray-like structure designed to hold paints and brushes.

Palette Knife

A tool, the working end of which is flat and round, used especially for applying thick layers of paint. See Impasto.

Palimpsest Effect

Images are superimposed on one another, perhaps indicating the passage of time or the exploration of preferences.

Panorama

An all-inclusive view of a wide landscape or a continuous scene such as action, historic event, or narrative.

It was a popular medium for the depiction of battle scenes of the Civil War and of American scenic views such as Niagara Falls. There developed a vogue for moving panoramas, with long strips of canvas wound on cylinders. A favorite was *The Burning of Moscow by Napoleon.* Sometimes the panoramas were accompanied by changing light and sound effects.

Papier Collé (pasted paper)

Originally a Chinese invention in the 10th century, it became a new art form in the hands of Braque and Picasso when they pasted materials, such as newspaper, cards, and wallpaper, flatly on canvas. It reflects a kind of liberation because the artist is free to compose or invent patterns and spatial qualities.

Papier Découpé (paper cutout)

A form of "drawing with scissors" by Matisse (1869-1954) when he created optical illusion with bands of color and colored form. He said: "Cutting to the quick in color reminds me of the sculptor's direct carving." Matisse used these designs for wall coverings, book illustrations, pictures, and priestly vestments.

Paper-cutting has been a Jewish art form since the 1100s. During holy days, homes are decorated with paper-cuttings facing east, the direction of Jerusalem.

Papier-Mâché

Strong but light molding paper pulped with glue and other substances, used most often in the construction of small and colorful sculptural creations. During centuries past, beginning A.D. 206, it was used especially for the production of useful items. Its use came into full flower during the Victorian era: elaborate, highly ornate objects in the decorative arts were created.

The resiliency of papier-mâché remained a popular alternative to expensive wood-carved ornamentation until the discovery of plastic in the 20th century.

Parergon

A glimpse of a detail (landscape, flowers, etc.) to give an added interest. See Detail.

Parfleche

In the Native American culture, a woman's art: abstract, dream-like designs are created on functional items such as knife sheaths, flat cases, and other objects.

Paris, School of

From the mid-1800s to the onset of WWII, the world of art revolved around Paris. Many of the major movements were formulated there. Its most well-known artists include:

Montcelli (1824-1886)
Puvis de Chavannes (1824-1898)
Boudin (1824-1898)
C. Pissarro (1830-1903)
Manet (1832-1883)
Degas (1834-1917)
Fantin-Latour (1836-1904)
Legros (1837-1911)
Sisley (1839-1899)
Cézanne (1839-1906)
Redon (1840-1916)
Monet (1840-1926)
Morisot (1841-1895)
Renoir (1841-1919)
H. Rousseau (1844-1910)
Gauguin (1848-1903)
van Gogh (1853-1890)
Bonnard (1867-1947)
Vuillard (1868-1940)
Matisse (1869-1954)
Denis (1870-1943)
Rouault (1871-1958)
Villon (1875-1963)
Vlaminck (1876-1958)
R. Dufy (1877-1953)
Léger (1881-1955)
Picasso (1881-1973)
Braque (1882-1963)
Modigliani (1884-1920)
Soutine (1894-1943)

Pastel Chalk or French Pastels

The ingredients of this soft, dry crayon consist of powdered pigment, chalk, and water mixed with gum. Pastel is regarded as a painting medium because its substance can be spread; it is especially suited for sketching and for rendering Impressionist works.

After many colors became available during centuries past, pastels were primarily used for making copies of oil paintings; during the late 1600s and the 1700s, this medium was considered ideal for portraiture. Classic is the work of Carriera (1675-1757) who used pastel for her portraits of many distinguished patrons in several countries. Chardin (1699-1779) developed the revolutionary technique now associated with pastel painting: layers of superimposed colors and broad hatching. H. Johnston (active 1705-1729), generally recognized as the first American female artist, brought the art of pastel from England to America. Degas (1834-1917) achieved a great and unusually refined mastery in this medium. The American Impressionist Twachtman (1853-1902) is renowned for his pastel technique.

Pastiche

The imitation of another artist's work; deceptive work.

Pastoral

A rural scene that may evoke a sense of nostalgia or a back-to-nature feeling.

Patina

The surface appearance of something grown beautiful over the years. Also, discoloration caused by exposure.

Patron of the Arts

See Art Patron.

Patroon Painters (1675-1750)

The first recognizable school of American art. The artists were influenced by English and Dutch styles, and specialized in portraiture. It was a common practice for artists to paint only the face from life and to copy the body from other works such as mezzotints. See Early American Art.

Pattern

1. A decorative, harmonious, or symbolic design.
2. A design created through the interplay and contrast of colors.

Pattern is particularly important in interior decoration (walls, floors, and ceilings), as well as decorative objects such as rugs and ceramics.

Pattern and Decoration or P & D (1970s)

A post-avant-garde movement in the tradition of De Stijl, Bauhaus, Art Nouveau, and Art Deco: a challenge to contemporary architecture and to interior design and decoration.

Kuchner (1949-   ) outlined its qualities: free communication, patterns (including prefabricated ones), and the motif secondary to visual effect. The artists wanted to concern themselves with the here-and-now in an attempt to change the public's taste with a wide range of influences: Islamic art, Mexican tiles, Moorish architecture, Pop art, and so on. They used bright, garish colors in decorative and ornamental paintings and furniture.

More recently, Kozloff (1942-) has created, for many public spaces, large tile and mosaic murals of startling color, decorative patterning, and complex detail, with pictorial allusions to local history and architecture.

Pattern Book

1. A medieval book which contained general forms of the human figure for use by painters and sculptors.
2. A book of motifs and designs used for reference by artists and industrial designers.

Peaceable Kingdom, The

Hicks (1780-1840), an eloquent Quaker preacher, turned for solace to the theme of his paintings: he created a vision of a "peaceable kingdom" in over 100 versions.

Peale Family, the

Its patriarch, Charles W. (1741-1827), sired 17 children, many of whom were outstanding artists, including Raphaelle (1774-1825), Rembrandt (1778-1860), Rubens (1784-1864), and Titian (1799-1885), who were named after master artists. Three artist-daughters were named after master artists Sofonisba Anguissola, Rosalba Carriera, and Angelica Kauffmann.

Charles' brother, James (1749-1831), another talented artist, was the father of five artists.

Aside from art, family members possessed diverse talents. They are regarded as the first family of Early American art. (As a note to history, there have been hundreds of families through the centuries whose members were multi-talented in the fields of painting, sculpture, architecture, and related fields.) See Museum and Pennsylvania Academy.

Peintres Maudits

A phrase used by art historians to describe those artists who lived wretched or desperate lives, and who suffered the most dreadful poverty, most notably Modigliani, Soutine, Utrillo, and van Gogh.

Peinture Claire

Painting light with a predominantly light tonality to suggest bright, outdoor color — a technique mastered by Boudin (1824-1898) and learned by the Impressionists from him.

Pennsylvania Academy of the Fine Arts

America's second oldest public gallery and art school. Prior to its establishment in 1805, the usual training ground for artists was Europe. The academy, now an art school and museum, has an outstanding collection of Early American paintings, particularly those of the Peale family. See Columbianum and Museum.

Pentimenti

1. The alterations made by an artist in the process of painting.
2. The re-appearance of drawings beneath the surface because of the aging of the canvas.

Penumbra

A shaded area between perfect shadow and full light.

Penwork (late 1700s-1840s)

This was a painting process applied to boxes, sewing tables, cabinets, fans, screens, and the like, but with so many formulas that "any definitions must come as generalizations that grow broader with the discovery of any new piece." The first step, generally, was to paint the object black. Patterns were then painted on in white gesso, and details then rendered in black India ink. Outlines of classical and pastoral scenes, with decorative borders, were popular subjects.

Perceptionism

A term coined by R.J. Anderson (1951-   ) for his landscape paintings that are the result of both objective and impressionist observations of nature. The artist's paintings are rendered in realistic colors, accented with bright highlights, and loose, swirling brushwork.

Performance Art (a time-based live art by visual artists) (1960s-1990s)

It has been called "the marriage of Conceptual art and Happenings." Specifically, theatre, music, and the visual arts are its main components. Generally, any subject, medium, or material is presented.

In 1977, 54 avant-garde artists presented Performances with several themes: the body, the senses, music, the spoken word, and so on. Another Performance was documented by diagrams, photographs, and interviews. Living Sculpture — when artists pose as statues — is another manifestation.

More recently, local events, environments, influences, and points of view have been expressed in Performances, with themes of personal experience, linguistic dialog, sexuality, politics, human rights, and ethnicity.

Performance Painting is a technique applied by artists Botello and Healty, who call themselves "The East Los Streetscrapers." Their paintings are done in public, in real time, for specific events: they paint in front of a playing band.

In the early 1990s, Blue Man Group (a trio of bald men painted blue) took everyday objects and realities and improvised a childlike blend of art and entertainment.

Personages

A series of 60 artworks created by Bourgeois (1911-   ), beginning in the 1940s: sculptures consist of totemic objects in wood and plastic.

Perspective

A technique perfected during the Early Renaissance: it applies a mathematical system to the portrayal of three dimensionality on a two-dimensional surface. Basically, it is a system where the illusion of reality is obtained. Several well-known types:

—Aerial or Atmospheric	Atmospheric conditions cause colors to lose their intensity and reduce color contrasts.
—Anamorphic	Referring to a distorted image which can be seen in true proportion if the painting is viewed from a certain point of view or in a curved mirror.
—Descriptive	An arrangement of figures according to importance of rank, a form used in ancient times.
—Foreshortening	The shortening of a single unit such as an arm or a leg. The discovery of foreshortening and of natural forms c. 500 B.C. by the Greeks was regarded as a great revolution in art.
—Linear	The use of converging lines.
—Oblique	To render an object turned at an angle.
—One Point	A figure near the vanishing point appears farther and smaller than a figure in the foreground.
—Reverse	It allows multiple points of view in one painting; figures also appear the same size anywhere in the painting.
—Skiagraphy	The correct gradations of light and shade in order to project shadows.

With his essays on form, shape, depth, and light, Piero della Francesca (1416-1492) is credited with developing theories of perspective.

Brunelleschi (1377-1446), an architect, whose work established a pattern for architecture for the ensuing 500 years, discovered linear perspective. This naturalistic effect became the basic element of European painting for the next five centuries. *The Holy Trinity* by Masaccio (1401-1428) is one of the first paintings made following the theories of perspective. See Space.

Petard

An artwork created to attract attention because of its strange color, composition, or theme.

Petroglyph

Engraving or painting images on pebbles, stones, and rocks was a common art form in prehistoric years.

Hundreds or, it is argued, thousands of years ago, Native Americans in Albuquerque, New Mexico, created some 17,000 religious etchings on volcanic rock. This area, called

Petroglyph National Monument, encompasses 7,200 acres.

In more recent times, petroglyphs have been created on rocks throughout the world by the artist Ken Hiratsuka, who said it was his purpose to leave a carving in every country to "symbolize that all nations share a similar point of view."

Phases (1950s-1960s)

The French poet E. Jaguer undertook to centralize the efforts of various countries and, with the publication of the periodical *Phases*, an international movement was formulated. Exhibitions were held throughout the world. The artists followed fundamental Surrealist principles: painting of the imagination. Humor and poetry were also important themes.

Philadelphia Centennial Exposition of 1876

Female artists, for the first time in the US, achieved public visibility: approximately one-tenth of art in the US section was by women.

Phillips Collection

Located in Washington, D.C., it is known as the oldest museum for Modern art in the US, having opened in 1921 for the purpose of showing the work of living artists.

Photo-Collage or Saff Tech

A special printing process used by Rauschenberg (1925-) in which the artist's photographs of construction workers, machinery, tools, and similar objects are first painted on special paper and then transferred onto sheets of wax. The wax image is then placed on canvas and more wax poured over it. The effect may be that of a laminated photograph or the image may appear to be an actual object encased in wax and suspended on canvas.

Photograms

A process conceived by Moholy-Nagy (1895-1946) when he began making abstract photographic images without a camera in the 1920s. His approach, rather than artistic, was scientific and technical. He thought he was making a breakthrough in communication. See Rayographs.

Photo-Impressionism

A term coined by Forbes (1948-) for his artworks which he paints with light bouncing off the surface of the pictures. He begins his paintings with photography and projects the slide to work from onto the white surface of a canvas. He proceeds from that point to create paintings reflecting city life.

Photomontage

Heartfield (1891-1968) claimed to have invented this Cubist-inspired technique, which is basically a kind of collage. It consists of photographically produced images from newspapers and magazines that are applied to a support to give the effect of film editing. This technique was used by the artist largely to fight for Germany's consciousness and soul. He used distortion and exaggeration in storylines to deride and ridicule Nazi rule and behavior, German traditions, current events, etc.

Another Dadaist, Höch (1889-1978), used photomontage specifically to caricature the political and social systems in Germany with both commentary and allegory: classic was her exhibition called "Cut With the Kitchen Knife Dada Through the Last Weimar Beer Belly Cultural Epoch of Germany."

Photomural

A very large, photographically produced mural applied to an interior surface. See Supergraphics.

Photo-Realism

An almost photographic technique: painstaking, clinical detail is the most outstanding feature of artworks that resemble painted photographs. Morley (1931-) was a pioneer of this technique when he started using as his models souvenir postcards of warships. Flack (1931-) began to compose enormous canvases, with colors filled in with an airbrush. Estes (1936-), another early experimenter, uses photographs of Manhattan cityscapes as models. The technique of Close (1940-) is to transfer the photographic image, detail by detail, onto a large canvas. See Post-Socialist Realism and Super-Realism.

Photo-Secession (1902-1910)

An association of American photographers formed by Stieglitz (1864-1946) in order to gain recognition of photography as a fine art. Steichen (1879-1973) was a founding member. See Art Photography and 291 Group.

Pictograph (picture writing)

1. A term used by archaeologists to describe hieroglyphs and ancient paintings or drawings on rock walls. They are among the earliest examples of a written language. In today's world, road signs are basic pictographs.
2. Several Abstract Expressionists were inspired and influenced by Native American art, which resulted in paintings similar to pictographs. Classic are the paintings of Gottlieb (1903-1974) who adopted a timeless, cross-cultural pictorial vocabulary in more than 300 pictographs derived from African, pre-Columbian, and American Indian artifacts and sculptures.

Picture Plane

The plane or space occupied by the surface of the picture.

Pietà

A title often used for paintings or sculptures of the dead Christ being held by Mary, most notably the sculpture rendered by Michelangelo, which is on view at St. Peter's in Rome. This religious motif evolved in Germany during the 1300s; it spread quickly to other European countries.

Pigment

A color derived from a powdered form obtained from the earth, stones, minerals, animals, vegetables, or chemicals.

Pittura Colta (cultivated painting) (1970s-1980s)

A term coined by the Italian critic I. Mussa to describe the post-modern work of Italian artists who employed academic technique and allegory in the creation of paintings that refer to Neoclassicism: a kind of mock classicism with allusions to the past.

Plasticity

1. The quality of three dimensionality in a plastic medium such as pottery or sculpture.
2. The semblance of three dimensionality attained through light, shadow, or content.

Pleinairism

An American movement, reaching full height during the 1880s, that sought to combine the atmospheric effects of natural light with academic technique. See American Landscape Painting and Luminism.

Plein-Air Painting

Referring to the painting of pictures out-of-doors to impart the quality of open air. Prior to the 1800s, the practice was to make sketches outdoors and to finish the work in studios. The Barbizon School, the Macchiaioli School, and the Impressionists were among the first to establish the practice of plein-air painting.

Pointillism

See Neo-Impressionism.

Polychrome Sculpture

Much ancient sculpture, as well as that of the medieval and Renaissance years, was multicolored in an attempt to make it more lifelike.

Polymorphic

The appearance of an artwork seems to change according to the viewer's position. See Kineticism.

Polyptych

1. An altarpiece consisting of a number of hinged panels on which a series of paintings is presented when the panels are opened or folded.
2. An artwork consisting of four or more parts.

Pompier Painting (l'art Pompier) (1860-1910)

Referring to paintings popular with the French Salons. These elaborate, highly colored artworks, with emphasis on mythological, medieval, apocalyptic, classical, or oriental scenes, appealed to the bourgeoisie. In time, however, they were relegated to flea markets; currently, they are regarded as high camp.

Pont-Aven Group

A group of artists who worked in Brittany under the charismatic leadership of Gauguin (1848-1903). The artists were preoccupied with the theory and practice of art. See Cloisonnism and Synthetism.

Pop Art (mid-1950s-1970s)

The impetus for this movement developed from discussions between English critics, sculptors, architects, and painters in the mid-1950s; they were interested in the new urban culture, especially as manifested in the US.

Basically, Pop has a dual quality: parody and the conversion of ordinary objects into "icons" when presented out of context. Appropriated images and artifacts from everyday life, the media, and traditional painting are fused with the techniques, colors, and scale of advertising art. This anti-high art resulted in a sophisticated "instant culture."

Although Pop artists shared the same attitudes of wit and irony, each developed a unique style or image.

There were many American, Canadian, English, and European Pop artists: Warhol (1928-1987) is probably the best known. See Post-Pop Art.

Pop Noir

A term coined by critics to describe an exhibition called "Helter Skelter: L.A. Art in the '90s." They were reminded of the dark side of life in urban America: black humor permeated disturbing works rife with themes of sex, violence, and rebellion.

Portfolio

1. A container for drawings or prints.
2. The artist's collection of works on paper.
3. In commercial art, a collection of the artist's work to be shown as a sample for sale or exhibition.

Portfolio Edition

A series of prints depicting one theme. The portfolio can be rendered by one artist or a group of artists. The prints may be sold separately or as a unit.

Portrait d'Apparat

In the portrait, the sitter's profession is suggested by apparel, accessories, or surroundings. Copley (1738-1815) developed a new approach to portraiture: a distinctive, momentary gesture, pose, or expression, sometimes accompanied by significant elements such as working clothes or the tools of one's profession or trade. Classic is a portrait of Paul Revere as a silversmith; this painting is regarded as a landmark in American art. See Cabinet Painting.

Portraiture

A painting, sculpture, drawing, or other artistic rendering of a person, living or dead; the capture of the essence of a person's facial features. That essence, however, is open to interpretation by the artist.

Aristotle defined three kinds of portraiture: the idealized, the naturalistic, and the satirical.

Although portraiture was practiced by the Egyptians, Greeks, and Romans, it was not until after the 1400s that depicting likenesses became a regular art form in the Western world. Among hundreds of portraitists, those who excelled include:

European

- van der Weyden (1400-1464)
- Clouet (1486-1540)
- Titian (1490-1576)
- Holbein (1497-1543)
- Tintoretto (1518-1594)
- Hals (1580-1666)
- Velásquez (1599-1660)
- Rembrandt (1606-1669)

English

- van Dyck (1599-1641)
- Reynolds (1723-1792)
- Cotes (1726-1770)
- Gainsborough (1727-1788)
- Wright (1734-1797)
- Beechey (1753-1839)
- Hoppner (1758-1810)
- Lawrence (1769-1830)
- Watts (1817-1904)
- John (1878-1961)

American

- Copley (1738-1815)
- Earl (1751-1801)
- Stuart (1755-1828)
- Trumbull (1756-1843)
- Rembrandt Peale (1778-1860)
- Sully (1783-1872)
- Sarah Peale (1800-1885)
- Bingham (1811-1879)
- Elliott (1812-1868)
- Eakins (1844-1916)
- Sargent (1856-1925)
- Henri (1865-1929)
- Rand (1876-1941)
- Kuhn (1880-1949)
- Speicher (1883-1962)
- Neel (1900-1984)

See Conversation Pieces, Donor Portraiture, Faiyum Portrait, Limners, National Work, Nude Portraiture, Portrait d'Apparat, and Self-Portrait.

Post-Avant-Garde Art

The world of commerce, mass media, and consumerism is the source of inspiration for the artist. Painting and photography, painting and sculpture, sculpture and architecture, photography and videographic imagery, etc., are mixed in multimedia displays. The artists have proven themselves as part of the media world of mass culture. See General Idea, Mass Art, and Media Artists.

Poster

A decorative bill for posting in public; an artistic rendition of an advertisement; a low-cost reproduction of a painting. The essentials of Poster art are clarity, simplicity, and timely or humorous theme. Its effectiveness depends on immediate visual impact, achieved through striking design and color. Toulouse-Lautrec (1864-1901) perfected

Poster art as it is known today: in his hands, the poster became a new art form. Several other artists who excelled were Penfield (1866-1925), Bonnard (1867-1947), Sloan (1871-1951), Beardsley (1872-1898), and Shahn (1898-1969).

Before the age of radio and TV, the poster was an important medium for getting messages across to the public, especially on the streets of large cities.

The master of commercial Poster art is Cappiello (1875-1942), who was responsible for the poster-symbol; in 1923, Cassandre (1901-1968) revolutionized this medium with surrealistic magic.

Recognizing that art is a powerful tool in the dissemination of ideas, posters became a primary form for the creation of agitation and propaganda ("agitprop") in the former Soviet Union and other revolutionary areas. Posters promoting war and revolution have been called "paper bullets" because they can be just as damaging as artillery. See Print and Printmaking.

Post-Impressionism (1880s-1906)

A term coined by the critic Roger Fry. He opined that the artists sought "to find a pictorial language appropriate to the sensibilities of the modern outlook . . . they do not seek to imitate form, but to create form."

Artists recognized as highly individual representatives of Post-Impressionism include Cézanne (1839-1906), whose intention was to paint the reality lying beneath the surface of the subject and to emphasize its form and structure, and van Gogh (1853-1890) and Gauguin (1848-1903), who were influential in their use of striking color, lack of symmetry, and ability to express themselves from their inner beings.

These three artists are regarded as the forerunners of Modern art in its various formats: Cézanne's work ultimately led to Cubism, van Gogh's to Expressionism, and Gauguin's to influence Symbolism. See Fauve Painting, Intimist Painters, Modern Art, Nabis, and Neo-Impressionism.

Post-Industrial Sculpture

A term coined in the 1980s to describe the work of several sculptors who, because of outdated technological developments, transformed industrial discards into three-dimensional "poetics of decay."

Classic is the work of Cragg (1949-) who gathered plastic throwaways to assemble them into sculptures such as the carpet-like floor piece, titled *New Stones-Newton's Tones*. Also, the work of Woodrow (1948-) who assembled discarded artifacts, such as mailboxes, world globes, and cameras, to create sculptures that resemble Duchamp's ready-mades.

Post-Minimalism or The New Sculpture (1967-1975)

A seemingly subverted and ephemeral art form suggestive of eccentricity and whimsy. Sculpture might be nothing more than rope, wire, neon tubing, rubber washers, ballbearings, or spilled paint. See Eccentric Abstraction.

Postmodernism

1. The current phase of a modernist tradition: a new, improved modernism.
2. A restatement of art of the past: a learned style.

3. A term used to characterize contemporary art and architecture. It is a new period and distinct from modernism.

Post-Painterly Abstraction

A term coined by the critic C. Greenberg in 1964 to designate the techniques of the generation of painters whose work departed from Abstract Expressionism. Essential characteristics include high-keyed, lucid color and linear clarity (hard-edge painting) on large, flat areas. The artists used color as both form and content.

Post-Pop Art

The integration of Pop art with the method and medium used by adult graffiti artists. Classic is the work of Crash (1962-); titles of watercolors include *The Vulture, Galactus,* and *Doctor Doom Profile.*

Post-Socialist Realism (sometimes called Hyper-Realism) (1970s)

Like Photo-Realist painters in the West, Soviet artists often depicted everyday life with almost photographic reality. Many of the artworks were found objectionable because they failed to advance the cause of communism.

Poussinism (Poussinisme)

The work of Poussin (1594-1665) was regarded as a model by 17th-century academic painters who thought the classical ingredients of drawing and design were fundamental and that color was only secondary. Admirers of Poussin were called "Ancients." See Rubenism.

Precisionism

See Cubist Realism.

Pre-Columbian Art

The art of North, Central, and South America from the period before the arrival of Columbus in America. Beginning c. 1250 B.C., two areas achieved the highest levels of cultural development: Mesoamerica and the Central Andes.

The societies of the first Americans were often complex, cosmopolitan, and sophisticated. The native peoples evolved a series of cultures, each unique and yet related to those who came before or after them.

Throughout the pre-Columbian world, art related to both religion and nature, as well as to secular power. Many of their sculptures, artifacts, and monuments have survived to impress us today.

Prehistoric

Referring to any past peoples who have left few clues to their culture, thereby preventing historians from creating a coherent picture of their development. Classic is the Paleolithic period of Europe when cave dwellers left drawings and paintings in caves. See Cave Art.

Pre-Raphaelism (1848-1862)

An esoteric reform movement in England. The artists wanted to depict the beauty of nature and humankind with sharply focused detail and luminous color. The key to their philosophy can be found in the writings of John Ruskin: true to nature and moral feeling.

Medieval, classical, and literary themes were stressed. They hoped to find simplicity and sincerity in the pure art of an age of faith long past: to return to the spirit of the medieval masters. Their works, however, are unmistakably English in appearance. Paintings were signed "P.R.B." (Pre-Raphaelite Brotherhood).

Presepio (crèche art)

In 17th- and 18th-century Naples presepio was the avocation of the age. It encompassed painting, sculpture, scenic design, and fashion. Both the sacred and the profane were presented in a mix of realism and fantasy. Ranging in size from eight to 18 inches, the puppet-like figures were noted for their lifelikeness and authentic dress. Scenes were designed with exact architectural detail and miniature accessories.

Primary Structures (sometimes referred to as Minimal Structures)

Sculptures of steel and concrete which are large enough to enable the spectator to walk through or around the artwork. In 1952/1953, a temporary museum (The Echo) was established in Mexico City by Goeritz (1915-1990), a constructivist sculptor, to house these gigantic, geometric structures. His ideas soon became internationally recognized.

Primitive

Natural; self-taught; simple; rudimentary.

Primitive Art

The art of an early period of a culture. In the context of surviving primitive societies of the New Stone Age (Africa, the Americas, and Oceania), it was concerned with the invisible world. In those societies, sculpture and art were intended for use in healing rituals, in magic, in ancestor worship, and in connection with the netherworld. Their seemingly distorted representations resulted from the belief that a living force came from God and filled the universe and all form. In essence, almost everything used in daily life was turned into a ritual art object to increase its efficiency or protective powers. Secular art did not exist and beauty was not a factor.

The role of carving was integral to daily life and important carvers were recognized as masters, equal to chiefs and other village heads.

During the early part of the 20th century, art from Africa played an influential role in the work of Picasso, Modigliani, and other modernists. (It was only after the publication of *Primitivism in Modern Art* in 1938 that African, Oceanic, and pre-Columbian art was regarded as serious art by historians.)

The tradition of Primitive art continues in Africa, but modern-day artists are not influenced by religion alone; symbolism and design have also become important motifs.

More recently, the contemporary world of art and sculpture has been divided into several categories, two of which are international (academically trained and city-based artists) and traditional (ethnographic motifs and artists who are village-based). Another category, urban art, is seen in commercial art with themes reflecting on the situations and realities of everyday life.

Primitives

A misleading term applied to painters during the 1300s (Trecento) and 1400s (Quattrocento), especially in Italy and the Netherlands.

Primitivism

1. As seen in cultures from millenniums past. See Primitive Art.
2. A term used to describe artworks that possess qualities of directness, simplicity, and boldness of color and image. See Naive Art.
3. The modernist attempts to embody qualities of primitivism in his work. See German Expressionism.

Print

This term is used in both original and reproduction art. For a print to be an original, the artist must do the plates or the stones. If someone else does the work, then it is a reproduction. (A print's value is partially determined by how involved the artist was in the creative process. Most often, the artist designs and prepares the matrix or surface from which the image is printed.)

Woodcuts, etchings, engravings, aquatints, lithographs, and serigraphs are forms of original prints. Each involves the artist's hand in drawing, brushing, or cutting. See Graphic Arts, Limited Edition, and Printmaking.

Printmaking

A series of techniques by which prints are produced, generally entailing etching or engraving an image on a plate, inking it, and then running it through a press for the purpose of producing a certain number of identical pieces called an "edition."

One kind of printmaking produces no more than one work, called a "monotype"; however, after the print is pulled from the surface, a residual image, called a "ghost," remains. The ghost may be re-inked or re-worked to produce a variation of the previous image or a further development of it. The full development of monotype as a medium culminated in the work of Degas (1834-1917).

Those artists or ateliers who have excelled in the techniques of printmaking are called "master printmakers." Whistler (1834-1903) was one of the most original, sensitive printmakers in history; classic are groups of etchings titled *The French Set, First Venice Set*, and *The Thames Series.*

In the 20th century, there were many American painter-printmakers who played vital roles in determining artistic developments and who treated printmaking as a major means of expression and communication, including, among others, Bellows, Benton, Davis, Hassam, Hopper, Lichtenstein, Marsh, Sheeler, Sloan, Warhol, and Wood. See Poster.

As a note to history, the first half of the 20th century is often described as the Golden Age of Printmaking: The Library of Congress has recorded over a thousand printmakers between 1900 and 1950, with emphasis on the 1930s, during the Great Depression.

Process Art (1960s-1970s)

An art form that grows during the period of creation. Its main criterion is perishability. Diverse raw materials (ice, grass, liquid, sawdust) are used and sited at random without structure and left to natural forces. The act of doing this is allegedly the art, rather than the end product. It seems to make a statement for life itself. See Conceptual Art.

Proportion

The application of rules which regulate the relationship of parts to the whole, used most often in depiction of the human figure. It is an important element in creating order, whether in a painting or sculpture representing beauty of form or expressive distortion.

Prouns (1920s)

A Russian acronym for "Project for the Affirmation of the New," coined by Lizzitsky (1890-1941) for his paintings which appear to be plans for imaginary cities. Geometric forms (the circle and the sphere, the square and the cube, the triangle and the pyramid) were used during this period of experimentation. Also, the creation of constructions which seem to be floating in space.

Provenance

The history of ownership of an artwork and a guarantee of its authenticity.

Pseudomachines

The kinetic assemblages created by Tinguely (1925-1991) are classic. Best known are his playful, noisy, and vibrating junk contraptions: radios, motors, and wheels were some of the materials of his artistic philosophy.

The term "dimensions variable" has been applied to the sculptures of Aycock (1946-); their parts have no fixed relationship and are adjustable. Her indoor works incorporate moving parts, flashing lights, and loud sounds. A typical work is *The Savage Sparkler*; standard industrial materials, such as fans, motors, sheet metal, steel, and heating coils, were used to create a useless machine. See Audiokinetic Sculpture and Machine-Art Performances.

Public Art

"Percent for Art" programs have been instituted by many city, county, and state governments, as well as by the federal government, and by other countries. Basically, a certain percentage of any budget allotted for public buildings is devoted to the installation of art, but always with the stipulation that it must suit the site for which it is intended. The choice of artist is made through the process of viewing slides of the work of many artists. The final decision is rendered by a panel of experts from the art world, along with participation of concerned public officials. See Mural.

In the 1990s, Public art is manifested, among other things, by "Culture in Action," a program in which neighborhoods participate in public events: spectacles and performances involving groups of people, a kind of social activism or community involvement. See Fluxus and WPA.

Public Buildings Administration (1939)
(known as Section of Painting and Sculpture in 1934 and as Treasury Section of Fine Arts in 1938)

This agency directed mural work on public buildings, contributed to the architecture and adornment of the New York World's Fair, and extended art programs to the Civilian Conservation Corps, among other works. See WPA.

Public Domain

A nonprofit organization dedicated to bringing the Naive paintings of New York City artist Fasanella (1914-1998) into public arenas because of his original themes on the American labor movement and his depiction of cityscapes and everyday scenes of American life. Through money raised by the sale of posters of the artist's work, original paintings were repurchased and placed where they can be seen by passing crowds.

Public Works of Art Project (1933-1934)

An agency created during the Great Depression to help poverty-stricken artists. It employed over 4,000 artists who produced approximately 15,000 works. See Federal Art Project.

Purism (1918-1925)

A kind of machine art established in Paris. Its founders, Ozenfant (1886-1966) and Le Corbusier (1887-1965), campaigned "for the reconstitution of a healthy art" reflecting the spirit of the age. They favored the adaptation of form to function; emotion and expression were excluded. They wrote the manifesto *After Cubism* (1918) in which they called on artists to use pure color and simple geometric form. Their theories had a strong influence on industrial design and architecture. See De Stijl and Suprematism.

Puteaux Group (1911-1914)

A discussion group led by Villon (1875-1963) and his brothers Duchamp (1887-1968) and Duchamp-Villon (1876-1918) to redefine the language of Cubism as practiced by Picasso and Braque. They criticized Analytical Cubism because it lacked human interest. Aside from the resolution of philosophical matters, new color harmonies were deduced and the aspects of modern-day life, most notably the machine, were brought into focus. *The Little Machine Shop* by Villon is classic of these new principles. The artists originated the Section d'Or movement. See Bateau-Lavoir Group.

Putti

Nude children, often winged, meant to depict angels and cupids, appeared in many Renaissance paintings and sculptures. They were originally seen in Greek and Roman art.

Q

Quadratura

The illusion whereby architectural decoration seems to extend a room into imaginary space. This technique reached full expression in Baroque Italy.

Quadro Riportato

A term describing easel pictures seen in normal perspective. They are inserted as ceiling decorations.

Quattrocento

Designating the 400s (1400s) during Renaissance.

R

Rangoli

An ancient, ephemeral, Indian art of floor painting, practiced solely by women. Patterns, designs, and materials used in this art form vary from region to region and from family to family. Common motifs and designs include geometric forms, elephants, goddesses, flowers, stars, and symbolic devices. Materials used can be flour, lentils, indigo powder, dyes, pebbles, etc.

Like modern movements in the Western art world, the emphasis is on creation — the goal is the process, not the object. See Conceptual Art and Process Art.

ROCI (Rauschenberg Overseas Culture Interchange) (1980s)

A multi-country project that sought to enhance international peace and understanding through art. For each location Rauschenberg (1925-   ) created new works inspired by the culture of the host country. Gifts of art were also given to the peoples of each country.

Rayographs (sometimes called Photograms)

Prints made by leaving objects on sensitized paper while exposed to light, without the use of a lens, were sometimes called "X-rays of the real world." Man Ray (1890-1976) has been referred to as "the great poet of the darkroom." His work was a strong influence on the development of art photography.

Contemporary photographers have recently revived this process to successfully achieve diverse and unusual effects: objects appear to record themselves directly, producing shadowy images and abstract patterns.

Rayonism (1911-1914)

A Russian adaptation to European avant-garde movements. Its manifesto stated: "Rayonism is the synthesis of Cubism, Futurism, and Orphism." Compositions were rays of light that intersected and dissolved in changing patterns; these luminous rays were called "lines of force." Larionov (1881-1964) and Goncharova (1881-1962), husband and wife, were its exponents.

Ready-Mades

A term coined by Duchamp (1887-1968) to describe preexisting elements as "works of art" which, in reality, were objects taken from everyday life. Their newness was reflected by new placement. Duchamp used these ready-mades as an attack on traditional art. He changed forever the meaning of contemporary art. See Post-Industrial Sculpture.

Realism

To represent the external world in an objective and factual manner: the antithesis of Ideal art. The philosophy called Positivism taught that only things that can be seen and heard are real; therefore, the artist was obliged to paint objects of nature in accurate detail and not to create anything from his imagination.

Courbet (1819-1877) responded to that philosophy when he turned away from the historical, mythological, and religious themes of European art that had lasted more than a thousand years. He theorized that railway stations, engine houses, mines, and factories were the miracles of the 19th century. His exhibition called "Le Réalisme" marked the revolution of nature and contemporary life becoming the artist's motifs. Only that which existed was important: the heroism of modern life and the problems of humankind became central themes.

Realism provided a vehicle for social protest, known as Social Realism.

In the US, Eakins (1844-1916) was one of the leading representatives of the worldwide movement of the realistic depiction of contemporary life. See Naturalism and Visual Realism.

Reattribution

In Museumspeak, the announcement that one or more of its famous artworks or treasured objects is in fact a fake.

Regionalism (1930s)

A movement based on art linked to the spirit of a place. It grew out of the desire to establish a genuinely American art by depicting American subject matter and to celebrate American regional life and history. Its basic doctrine was that an artist should paint what he knows best: his home territory. Many regionalist paintings extolled the rugged virtues of homespun life.

Regionalism may be regarded as the Midwestern branch of American Scene Painting. It is associated largely with the work of Benton (1889-1975), Wood (1892-1942), and Curry (1897-1946), who did a great deal of painting on local themes. In the Southwest, centered in New Mexico, painters dealt with landscape and the life of Native Americans. See Taos/Santa Fe School.

In a general sense, consistent painting of any local area can be termed Regionalism. See Western and Indian Painting.

Regulating Lines

Geometric forms and proportions which are used as a "visual language" in painting.

Relief

Its techniques include:

—Shallow	Built-up area of impasto or other medium.
—Bas or low	Cameo in which the background is cut away or Intaglio in which the design is below the surface.
—Demi or half	The dimensions of depth are roughly half that of low and high relief.
—Haute or high	A sculpture from which at least half of the surface projects.

Relief sculpture — executed in varying degrees of depth against a two-dimensional background — has a long tradition, dating back to the ancient world and the

Renaissance. This art form was revived in the 1800s in Europe and introduced to the US primarily through the work of expatriate artists. By the late 1800s, relief sculpture had become a popular alternative to the portrait bust.

Remarque

A pencil drawing done by the artist in the margin of an offset print. Since it is an original work, it greatly enhances the value of the reproduction.

Renaissance (1420-1580)

It was the first period in history to be aware of itself and to give itself a name. Basically, it was a period of the rebirth of knowledge and culture in Europe, especially in Italy, under the aegis of classical art and literature. (Italians idealized the classical past, seeing their own period as a second Golden Age.) It was an age of discovery in perspective and knowledge of the classical form of architecture by the Italian masters. In painting, the canons of harmony and proportion were recognized and interpreted; mastery of technique developed.

The rules of art criticism also developed, whereby the criteria of good and bad art were modeled on classical tradition.

Art, on the whole, was Christian in its roots and in its meaning, and "true moral philosophy" was required of the artists.

Florence was the seat of the Renaissance shortly after 1400. See Early Renaissance, High Renaissance, and Humanism.

Renaissance Man or Universal Man

A term of esteem given to a person who is expert and multi-talented in several areas, especially in intellectual activity and in the arts.

Leonardo da Vinci is regarded as the embodiment of the Renaissance man. As a painter, sculptor, and architect, his artistic sensibilities enabled him to make original discoveries and inventions in academic and scientific fields.

Replica

See Copy.

Repligraphy (1990s)

A process that produces a new kind of original art without using offset printing. The image is reproduced as a photographic transparency and a new emulsion is made on an oil-based film. The emulsion is then fused onto the canvas. A new copy of the emulsion is used for each piece of canvas. Thereafter, each reproduction is hand-retouched by the artist with oil paint and then signed and numbered. By C.R.A. Productions Lab, California. See Artagraphy.

Repoussoir (to push back)

1. A compositional device, such as a figure or object, placed in the foreground so that all other details are seen beyond it.
2. The use of dull colors around bright colors, or the reverse, so as to achieve the illusion of depth.

Representational Painting

The depiction of a recognizable subject. It may or may not be realistic.

Retablo

Since colonial times, Mexicans have commemorated divine intervention at critical times, and for occasions of misfortunes escaped, with miniature paintings. Painted on fabric, paper, tin, or wood, these works, also called ex-voto paintings, depict both the event and the holy agent of miraculous salvation. In more recent times, photographs have also been used. See Ex-Voto and Santos.

Retro-Futurism

Referring to design that reflects both tradition and modernism (the past and the future), a term especially applicable to Japanese products.

Revolutionary Art

During the 1700s/1800s, Goya (1746-1828) and Daumier (1808-1879) rendered thousands of caricatures commenting on the evils of political life, the abuses of society, and the cruelty and injustice perpetrated against the common people who struggled with poverty and oppression.

In Germany, Kollwitz (1867-1945), a political graphic artist, sketched poor working women, showing them as revolutionaries in her series on the Peasants' War. She used forceful images of women and children to illustrate socialist and pacifist concerns. See Social Realism and War Art.

In Mexico, the work of Los Tres Grandes resulted in a multitude of murals depicting modern production, social criticism, and revolution. More particularly, the frescoes of Rivera (1886-1957), regarded as the most famous Mexican artist, depict scenes from the lives of heroic, landless peasants and their struggles for land reform, labor rallies and strikes, historical moments, visions of Mexico's lost history, caricatures of greedy capitalists, and portraiture of political figures.

Rocky Mountain School

See Hudson River School.

Rococo (1730-1780)

As a refined outgrowth of and a reaction to Baroque, it made its first appearance in France and was, above all, a style of interior decoration.

In painting, it was a decorative style marked by curving line, soft contour, soft light, and bright color. Two themes evolved: (a) the depiction of sensual or frivolous subjects and (b) genre scenes depicting in exaggerated form the value of domestic virtues.

In England, Rococo had the effect of bringing about the first important school of painting in decades.

In Italy, Rococo was represented by the work of Venetian artists.

During this period, there was great activity in the creation of smaller decorative objects. Classic are the porcelain figures made under the hand of Bustelli (1723-1763) in France and the carved wooden statues of Gunther (1725-1775) in Germany. See Neoclassicism.

Roman Art

The Greco-Roman period (145 B.C.- A.D. 400) was actually an extension of the Classical period of Greece. (The world's museums are full of Roman copies of Greek originals.)

Greek ideas extended to architecture, including town-planning, and the creation and adornment of interiors. The Pantheon, the Roman Forum, and the Colosseum are classic.

Important achievements in the art world were portrait busts, narrative relief, still lifes, fresco painting, and coins; portraiture came to be associated with worldly fame and power. Funerary monuments and statuary were intended to preserve exact likenesses of decedents; ordinary Romans, in fact, left a remarkable record of themselves in the form of tombs, tomb sculptures, and epitaphs. The deceased had themselves sculpted on tombstones as they appeared in various aspects of their lives.

The pictorial arts are among the most significant elements in the artistic legacy of Rome. Thousands of frescoes (mythological subjects, narrative, and landscapes) were recovered chiefly in Herculaneum and Pompeii where, as the result of the eruption of Vesuvius (A. D. 79) a protective coating formed on the painted walls. Excavation of the ruins began in 1719.

There were many silversmiths. Producing mosaics was a major industry and no important building was complete without them.

Romanesque (A.D. 950-1150)

Romanesque means of expression were those of the sacred. Manuscript illumination and fresco painting were the traditional art forms. Monks and laypersons were busy with the minor arts: goldsmiths, ivory carvers, tapestry weavers, and enamel, glass and ceramic workers created thousands of beautiful objects.

This period of culture was also very productive of impressive sculpture and the construction of churches. Durham Cathedral in England and the church of Santiago de Compostela in Spain are classic.

Romanesque sculpture, including bas-relief, has been called "the first step in representational art." See Gothic and Ottonian Renaissance.

Romanists

Flemish artists of the 1500s who were drawn to and influenced by the arts and antiquities of Rome.

Romanticism (1790s-1830s)

A representational style that influenced art of the imagination, with literary, historical, and religious themes leading the way. The artists triumphed in beauty, exotic places, dramatic action, and strong colors. Delacroix (1798-1863), a leading exponent of Romanticism, said: "What I demand is accuracy for the sake of imagination."

Copley (1738-1815) and West (1738-1820), both Anglo-Americans, were imaginative re-creators of the times. *Watson and the Shark* and *The Death of General Wolfe* are classic of the romantic trend. See Tableau d'Histoire.

Majestic landscape, in general, emerged, especially in England, Germany and the US. See Hudson River School.

Rotorelief

A disc modeled on a phonograph record. When "played," the design would give the illusion of disappearing into itself. Duchamp (1887-1968) and Man Ray (1890-1976) were the innovators of this technique. See Dada.

Rubbings

The placing of tracing papers over brass plaques and rubbing them with a substance to obtain a direct impression. See Frottage.

Rubenesque

A description of figures, painted by Rubens, because of their fullness and curves.

Rubenism (Rubenistes)

A school of thought in France during the 1600s/1700s which held that color was as important as design — that color was the essence of life and nature. Admirers of Rubens (1577-1640) were called "Moderns." See Poussinism.

Russian Style (1750-1917)

A national art movement that incorporated religious and secular themes, including folk art and craftwork, into church and domestic architecture, as well as into the decorative, graphic, and fine arts.

S

Sacra Conversazione (holy conversation)

A type of painting that enjoyed popularity during the Renaissance: the Madonna and Child are enthroned and surrounded by saints so that all the figures appear to have some emotional relationship. Classic is *The Virgin and Child with Saints* by Giovanni Bellini (1430-1516). See Maestá.

Sacred Spaces

A contemporary, international exhibition group whose spiritual representations are depicted in various media. The major theme is to demonstrate the symbology employed by artists through the ages in relation to spiritual matters.

Salon d'Automne (1903-1914)

Established in France by a group of painters, poets, and critics who were dissatisfied with the juried conservatism of the academic Salons and the anarchy of the Indépendants with no juries at all. The organizers solved the jury problem by selecting members by lot. Among its members were Renoir, Vuillard, the Fauve painters, and the Cubists.

This Salon was another milestone in 20th-century art.

Salon des Refusés (1863)

An exhibition set up by Emperor Napoleon III to display the work of artists who had been refused by the official academy. This Salon has been referred to as the turning point from which to begin the history of Modern art.

Salon Painting

France's annual official art exhibition was established in 1667. The Salon encouraged immaculately finished, conventional paintings, often on historical, religious, and mythological subjects, as well as formal portraiture. Recognition in the annual Salon was the most effective way for an artist to establish himself. See Academy Art and Pompier Painting.

Sand Painting

For more than 2,500 years, Tibetan Buddhist monks have created colorful designs, called "mandalas," that are the makings of a unique religious art: the mandala serves as a map of the inner reality that guides one to spiritual awareness. Funnels are used to direct grains of sand onto prepared symmetrical designs that symbolize harmony of the universe; thereafter, the mandalas are dismantled at religious ceremonies.

Native Americans of the Navajo tribe have created paintings in the sand in connection with healing rites.

The Surrealist Masson (1896-1987) invented a new form of sand painting when he spread glue over the canvas, poured colored sand over it, and then drew over it with paint squeezed directly from the tube.

Santos (holy figures)

One type of religious art, combining Native American and Spanish traditions, that thrived in colonial New Mexico, especially in the northern part where it ruled supreme from 1600 to 1850.

By petitioning for aid through the santos (either retablos, painted on flat supports, or bultos — wooden, polychromed sculptures in the round), the faithful expected the saints, who were sometimes accompanied by certain attributes, to perform deeds. (They also served as adornments.)

Regarded as a group, classical New Mexican santos were created between 1780 and 1907: the golden age for santeros (carvers) witnessed the birth of a new American Folk art. Modern santeros are still at work.

The modernist Hartley (1877-1943) produced a series of paintings focusing on santos.

Sarcophagus

These carved-stone coffins were decorated with narrative relief; subjects were varied and depicted in a realistic or abstract manner. Classic is a general's sarcophagus which might allude to his prowess in military affairs and also to the soul's triumph after death. Quite often, a sculpted representation of the decedent was attached to the lid. *The Good Shepherd*, a blend of pagan and Christian symbolism, was popular among Early Christians; it appears on many sarcophagi and in catacomb paintings. See Funeral Monuments and Roman Art.

Scagliola

A marble-like mixture of gypsum, pigment, and glue which is used as a filler for incised design on desks, tables, boxes, and similar objects, as well as for framed pictures.

This technique for creating faux inlaid marble dates back to Egypt, but was used extensively during the Renaissance. Its use has been revived in Europe and the US.

Scale

The comparison of the size of the painted or sculpted subject to realistic size.

Scale Life

Life-size, full-length portraits. See Academy Figure.

Scheme

The basic proportions for the drawing of objects to conform to appearance, based on the canons of proportion from ancient times and antiquity, but developed into a simplified schemata following Renaissance research.

School

1. Comprised of a geographical area (national, regional or local).
2. A following, especially applicable to the Middle Ages when certain masters had their own shops or when certain cities had their own groups of artists.
3. Artists working together who create an inventive atmosphere.

4. Artists who know each other: they often work in neighboring studios and use the same techniques.
5. When a term such as "School of Paris" is used, it means the art produced in Paris by artists who worked or studied there.

School of Chatou (1900-1904)

The artists Vlaminck (1876-1958) and Derain (1880-1954) rendered paintings characterized by bright colors and bold brushstrokes; their work became the harbinger of Fauve painting.

School of Fontainebleau (1500s)

A term associated with artists who worked in the court at Fontainebleau. Francis I wanted to honor the French crown by instituting a revival of the arts. He brought in Italian masters to initiate this revival, most notably Rosso (1494-1540), Primaticcio (1504-1570), and dell'Abbate (1512-1571), who were assisted by French and Flemish artists.

School of Leyden (1600s)

Referring to those painters in Holland who rendered meticulous genre scenes.

School of London

A title coined by the artist Kitaj in 1976 to designate those artists seeking to establish a native tradition in painting. Two views of this school: (a) foreign-born, figurative artists who have worked in London for decades and (b) artists who represent the development of a national tradition from the early 1900s up to, and including, the current decade.

School of the South (El Taller Torres-Garcia) (1937-1962)

The modern Latin American workshop established by the Uruguayan artist Torres-Garcia (1874-1949), who wanted to develop a new visual language: experimentation with diverse materials and innovative techniques, as well as tradition, in the creation of abstract paintings, sculptures, ceramics, wood and iron reliefs, constructions, murals, architectural projects, and furniture. This new artistic era bridged the gap between the Old and New Worlds: the combination of avant-garde works with the symbols and structures of ancient civilizations.

This school has been called the most significant Latin American art-education community of its time.

School of Winchester (900s-1100s)

One of the great schools of manuscript painting of the Middle Ages. These imaginative English artists produced a new excitement with renderings that seem to vibrate with life.

Scrimshaw

A carved or engraved functional or decorative object, with strong nautical association, made from solid materials such as whalebone, whale ivory, wood, metal, or shells.

Scriptorium

A communal room during medieval years, in monasteries all across Europe, in which nuns or monks dedicated themselves to the copying, illustrating, and binding of books. In today's world, Electronic Scriptorium, a private company, employs monks and nuns to computerize records and catalogs.

Sculpitecture

A term coined by Caro (1924-) for his sculptures which resemble architecture: viewers walk around the artworks and sometimes enter their cutout interiors.

Sculpto-Pictoramas by Grooms (1937-)

Referring to paintings, assemblages, constructions, and environments in which entire rooms are filled with cutout figures and replicas of buildings, bridges, public transit, and many other objects, all painted in brilliant and clashing colors. These artworks are characterized by whimsy, wild fantasy, and slapstick humor which are rooted in popular, contemporary culture. The viewer is confronted with a fun-filled environment of images that seem to be continually happening. Titles of these fields of action include *City of Chicago*, *Ruckus Manhattan*, and *Ruckus Rodeo*.

Sculpture

Its major techniques include (1) carved (cutting up), (2) modeled (building up), and (3) assembled (the joining or construction of prefabricated elements). Its three dimensionality creates volume, mass, and presence in space. Common materials used include bronze, clay, fiberglass, marble, plaster, stone, wire, and wood. Among its masters:

G. Pisano (1245-1314) and N. Pisano (active 1258-1278), who founded a great school of sculptors

Ghiberti (1378-1455)
Donatello (1386-1466)
Michelangelo (1475-1564)
Cellini (1500-1571)
Bernini (1598-1680)
Houdon (1741-1828)
Rodin (1840-1917), the father of modern sculpture
Pompson (1855-1923)
Brancusi (1876-1957)
Young (1877-1957)
Archipenko (1887-1964)
Lipchitz (1891-1973)
Moore (1898-1986)
Nevelson (1899-1988)
Savage (1900-1962)
Giacometti (1901-1966)
Hepworth (1903-1975)
David Smith (1906-1965)
Manzù (1908-1991)
Bourgeois (1911-)
T. Smith (1912-1980)
Caro (1924-)
J. S. Johnson (1930-)
Marisol (1930-)
Bontecou (1931-)
Graves (1940-1995)
DeAndrea (1941-)

Sculptural Walls

An art form practiced by Nevelson (1899-1988), who constructed reliefs from boxes and compartments filled with abstract assemblages, which were pointed gold, white, or black. Her more recent constructions were created with a variety of materials such as aluminum, steel, and Lucite. Critic S. Tillim described this artist as "an action painter with solids."

Scumbling

The skimming of a rather thin layer of lighter paint over either a translucent or opaque layer of darker paint, which alters the original color.

Seascape Painting

A popular art during the 1800s. The sea was the great unknown and, as such, man's respect and fear of it were expressed in action-filled paintings depicting historic or romantic shipwrecks, battles, whaling expeditions, and the effects of weather. Birch (1779-1851) is often referred to as the founder of this genre. See Marine Painting.

Secession (Sezession) (1890s-early 1900s)

Basically, this title refers to certain exhibition associations in Austria and Germany such as the Berliner Sezession in 1898 and the Neue Sezession in 1910. Perhaps the Vienna Secession in 1897 is the most memorable because one of its founders was Klimt (1862-1918); he was a master of decorative, flat-patterned painting.

The artists themselves were in the avant-garde; they were interested in the latest developments in painting and the decorative arts. Symbolism and Expressionism were primary motifs.

Section d'Or (Golden Section) (1912-1914)

This was an experimental Cubist exhibition group. The artists declared their independence from the domination of Braque and Picasso.

Three motifs permeated their work: the attempt to express movement, the expanding use of color, and use of the techniques of Cubism in Abstract art. See Puteaux Group.

Self-Portrait

A rendering of the artist's own likeness. In most instances, self-portraits disclose the character, spirituality, and emotions of the artists. Classic are the self-portraits Rembrandt (1606-1669) made over a period of 40 years; they constitute a revealing autobiography. The German artist Corinth (1858-1925) rendered 60 self-portraits in which the course of aging is depicted, along with expressions of intense emotion. Schjerfbeck (1862-1946), a Finnish modernist, created 40 expressive self-portraits. The German graphic artist Kollwitz (1867-1945) rendered over 100 self-portraits that reveal the accumulated effects of her hardships and sorrows. The German painter Beckmann (1884-1950) portrayed himself about 80 times in a range of roles, both earthly and divine.

A more up-to-date version is by the photographer Gorgoni whose photographs of well-known contemporary artists have been enlarged and applied to canvas. The artists themselves have altered the images to reflect their own moods. Another modernist is Rova (1958-) whose self-portrait is an oversize, three-dimensional head built with brightly colored wire: various mechanical devices within represent activities of the brain and head. See Auto-Iconography and *Vollard Suite*.

Semiotics

In today's world, it involves the theory of analyzing signs and symbols. Gestures, imagery, nonlinguistic sounds, and coded words are endowed with abstract meanings: the truth of hidden language is revealed. Classic are the semiotics of advertising and marketing in which language and imagery have an immensely powerful effect.

Serial Art, Serial Imagery, or One-Image Art

In its simplest form, it ranges from copies of antique statues to reproduction of multiples. In other works, it may be related by a common subject or theme: an art form conceived as a series with identical, similar, or different versions of the same subject, or rendered with different materials or colors. In most cases, each part of the series is incomplete: all the pieces together act upon one another. The latter technique was often used by Warhol (1928-1987) in painted canvases and photographic images in which he portrayed the same subject repeatedly, with only slight variations in composition, as in the *Campbell Soup Can* series or as in portraiture.

In 1976, Peter Max (1937-) began his annual tradition of painting *Liberty*. (These portraits led directly to the restoration of the Statue of Liberty in 1986.)

Sfumato

The blending of light and dark tones in order to create a soft, delicate effect. This technique is attributed to Leonardo da Vinci.

Shade Picture

A profile portrait usually cut out of shaded paper: a silhouette.

Shâh-Nâmeh (Book of Kings)

An illustrated epic poem of more than 50,000 rhyming couplets recounting the legends and traditions of ancient Iran, and regarded as the greatest artwork ever created in Iran. When it was created in the 1500s, it contained 258 painted miniatures and 759 illuminated pages. Because pages have been sold separately through the years, art circles consider it one of the most appalling acts of vandalism since WWII. Many of the pages were recently returned to Iran.

Shaped Canvas (1950s-1960s)

The extension of painting into the third dimension when easel painting takes on the appearance of a sculpted form because of the shape of the canvas. It opened the way for new approaches to pictorial structure, most notably in the work of Newman (1905-1970), Noland (1924-), and Stella (1936-). (As a note to history, artworks have always been created on nonrectangular supports such as altarpieces, tondi, and works made in conjunction with architecture.)

Ship Portraits

See Marine Painting.

Shodo

The Japanese style of calligraphy practiced by a large populace. Balance, rhythm, grace, and the beauty of line are its inherent qualities and, at its highest level, Shodo is perceived as a spiritual means of cultivating one's personality by developing integration of mental and physical energy.

Show Figures

During the 1800s, life-size wood and metal street sculptures were used to advertise business establishments; most popular was the "cigar store Indian." More than 5,000 show figures once populated the streets of New York City alone.

Sienese School

Duccio (1260-1319)
P. Lorenzetti (1280-1348)
Martini (1285-1344)
A. Lorenzetti (active 1319-1410)
Barna (active 1330-1360)
Bartolo (1330-1410)
DiBartolo (1370-1428)
Domenico (1400-1447)
DiPietro (1406-1481)

Signature Style/Image

The repetitive use or representation by an artist of an image, color, or contour or the use of a process, material, or medium that helps the viewer to attribute the work.

Signed and Numbered

The total number of impressions contained in a limited edition, authenticated by the artist's signature and the order in which the impression is signed: 5/100 indicates the fifth print out of an edition of 100.

Hand-signing prints became a custom during the second half of the 1800s. By 1915, the current custom of indicating the size of the edition and the number of the print began, exclusive of trial proofs, printer's proofs, artist's proofs, and a bon-à-tirer. By the late 1960s, artists and publishers added refinements indicative of a first, second, or third edition (A 1/100, B 1/100, C 1/100). A posthumous edition is one printed from a matrix after the artist's death.

Silhouette

A term referring to small portraits or outlines of objects either on solid black or white; it was a popular art form in the late 1700s/early 1800s.

Simplified Form

Form is reduced to its basic essentials.

"Simplified" Impressionism

The practice of Dove (1880-1946) in transforming his subjects into broad areas of color with the use of an optical projector.

Simultaneity

A method of depicting movement through repetition of superimposed images. See Futurism.

Simultaneous Representation

The portrayal in a picture of more than one view of a subject.

Sistine Chapel (The Vatican) (1508-1512)

The site for a series of murals depicting biblical stories. This masterpiece by Michelangelo of the Florentine School has been described as the greatest art ever done by man and is regarded as a tribute to the beauty of man and his redemption. Michelangelo's abilities seemed to be divinely inspired and life enhancing; he was called "il divino."

Site-Specific Art

A painting, sculpture, or other artistic endeavor that is created specifically for a certain site in a designated area. For centuries artworks — from Michelangelo's Sistine Chapel frescoes to Diego Rivera's murals — have been site-specific. See Mural and Public Art.

Situationist International (l'International Situationiste) (1957-1972)

A kind of anti-art movement composed of painters, writers, architects, and film makers who were active in several European countries; they also published a semi-annual journal. Videos, documents, models, canvas, and posters were some of the vehicles of expression used to expose and criticize the situations, ideas, and spectacles of modern life. See Dada and Fluxus.

Sketch

An unstudied or spontaneous drawing or painting usually employed as a draft for a finished painting or sculpture.

Its major approaches are the working sketch or study (a kind of memorandum) and the sketch that records the artist's direct impression (although not a completed picture, it is an end in itself).

Sketch Box

A small box used for carrying painting equipment, including palette, brushes, tubes, and turpentine.

Sketches

A series of 200 watercolors rendered by Miller (1810-1874) from 1858 to 1860 when he was commissioned to capture the Western scene; his approach to portraiture of Native Americans and to landscape was romantic and picturesque. See Indian Gallery.

Social Expressionism

A term coined by R.W. White (1951-) to describe a series of artworks, called *Artifacts from the Street*, created by him from collaged life-size photographs, plywood, housepaint, and the like. In association with Comic Relief, an organization dedicated to helping homeless families, he has joined with social service agencies to depict the plight of the homeless.

Socialist Realism

Realistic depiction of the life of the working class was a primary subject in the former Soviet Union, including utopian Stalinist policies of achievements in the arts, sciences, and sports; the construction of factories, mills, and power stations; the development of new railways and waterways; the mechanization of collective farms; and the erection of housing units.

When the communists took control of artistic life, they abolished avant-garde experimentation: uniform expression of the communist ideal was demanded. The party's maxim for artists was to demand "the truthful, historically concrete portrayal of reality in its revolutionary development": Socialist Realism was declared the "new and highest stage in the development of man's artistic ability."

Celebration of the paradise that communism would bring was the common theme, along with portraiture of Red Army leaders and other personages of the Revolution. See Degenerate Art and Post-Socialist Realism.

Social Realism

In this branch of Realism, focus is on social abuses and inequities: it commonly deals with problems of contemporary life and is sometimes accompanied by similar ideas in literature, theatre, film, and music.

Classic is the work of Young (1866-1943), who protested child labor and championed women's suffrage and racial equality, and the work of Shahn (1898-1969), who rendered a series of 23 gouaches on the theme of the *Sacco-Vanzetti* case. See Ash Can School, The Eight, and Revolutionary Art.

Society of Six (1917-1929)

A group of plein-air painters in Northern California who applied color in bold, bright flashes of painterly Expressionism. Their paintings of the landscape, the rural environment, and of figuration seem to explode with vibrant color, light, and earthly vitality. Part of their informal manifesto: "Seeing is the greatest joy of existence, and we try to express that joy."

Gile (1877-1947)
Clapp (1879-1954)
Logan (1886-1977)
Gay (1890-1970)
von Eichman (1899-1970)
Siegriest (1899-1989)

Soft-Edge or Soft-Focus Painting

Curved or gentle image: a tactile, caressing style conveying a suggestion of unity and fluency. See Hard-Edge Painting.

Soft Sculpture

One of the specialties of Oldenburg (1929-) is to stuff cloth and vinyl to create boldly colored, humorous replicas of common items such as bathtubs, typewriters, and drums. His intention was to humanize the products of industrial society and to give them a host of meanings — ironic or witty connotations, as well as serious social comment. See Pop Art.

Ringgold (1930-) is known for free-standing soft sculptures: *Harlem 76*, portraying Harlem street life; the *Couples* series, portraying the problems of courtship and family life. See Black American Art.

Solid Forms

Geometric forms (cubic/sphere) having three dimensions. See Form.

Solid Painting

Painting with a loaded brush or palette knife to build up with impasto.

Sotto in Sù

The extreme of illusion in foreshortening which shows figures, painted on a ceiling, that seem to be floating in space. See Perspective.

Space

In one, two or three dimensions, a limited extension in distance, area, or volume. The simplest and oldest type of space is two dimensional, which lacks perspective. Naturalistic or optical space relates to how things are perceived — a method perfected during the Early Renaissance as perspective. It remained the standard until Cézanne and those following him attempted to modify or abolish it.

Space Exploration

Outdoor installations created by Miss (1944-) in which the disciplines of sculpture, architecture, engineering, and landscape design are brought together. These environmental pieces permit viewers to physically explore the installation and to probe its spatial effects. Classic is her landscaped walkway located in Battery Park City in lower Manhattan. See Environmental Sculpture.

Spiral (1960s)

A group of about 15 black American artists who gathered together periodically to "discuss their position in American society and to explore other common problems." It was the opportunity to speak of a cultural self.

Sport in Art

The bond between art and sport is an enduring one: many memorable images have been recorded by artists who found sport an attractive subject. The first types of visual expression are the hunting scenes painted on cave walls. Athletes and athletic contests were portrayed by the Greeks in vase painting and sculpture. Pre-Columbian sports were depicted in murals, bas-reliefs, drawings, and statuettes. During medieval years, hunts and tournaments were the subjects of tapestries and illuminated manuscripts. The depiction of horse races and other equine activities was common in Great Britain.

In more recent times, many of the world's museums count among their collections sporting art by such renowned artists as Bellows, Degas, Eakins, Eastman, Goya, Homer, Remington, Stubbs, and Tait. Boxing and baseball are two sports that have provided many painters and sculptors with magnificent subject matter. Other sports include boat races, fishing, outdoor games, swimming, and rowing.

In today's world, serious treatment of various activities, such as basketball, car racing, football, golf, skiing, surfing, and major sporting events like the Olympics, have been rendered by many artist-athletes. The paintings are usually reproduced in limited editions.

Stabile

A term coined by the artist Arp to describe the large abstract sculptures of Calder (1898-1976). They have no moving parts and give the appearance of being rooted in place. See Mobile.

Stained Glass

A craft which involves the use of small pieces of colored glass to create designs, patterns, or narrative. The craft of creating stained-glass windows in the Western world is of Byzantine origin and has been used predominantly in the service of Christianity. By the 1100s, during the Gothic period, the French had developed it into one of the most distinctive forms of medieval art. This period is especially known for the beauty of its stained glass.

More recently, Clarke (1953-) has rendered huge, architecturally artistic stained-glass designs for buildings and other structures throughout the world. Several of his luminous projects include a shopping center in Japan, stage sets, and a country club.

Of all kinds of glass art, none is more widespread and enduring than stained glass. After blossoming in medieval times, this medium declined in popularity, then came back to prominence in the late 1800s.

Old and New Masters have designed stained-glass windows. See Art Nouveau.

Stain Painting, Color Painting, or Color Field Painting

A soak-stain technique developed by Frankenthaler (1928-) that made possible a new kind of painting, without brushwork. She poured thinned acrylic paint onto unprimed, unstretched canvas. The paint soaked into the canvas which was then folded; the colors would flow. See *Veils*.

Stela

A carved or inscribed stone slab or pillar used for commemorative purposes. Classic is a collection of almost 1,100 tablets, many as high as ten feet, incised with classical, philosophical texts, located in Xian, China. UNESCO has designated this collection as one of the world's great art treasures.

De Stijl (The Style) (1917-1931)

This movement, formed in Holland by Mondrian (1872-1944) and van Doesburg (1883-1931), began with publication of the magazine *De Stijl.* The artists hoped to develop "a new awareness of beauty." They wanted to help modern man become receptive to new developments in the arts with writings by the artists themselves.

De Stijl was a considerable influence on European and American visual art, architecture, and design in the area of posters, typography, furniture, fashions, and interiors. Mondrian's influence has been strongly felt; his work is part of the continuing past.

The style of painting practiced by Mondrian, along with van der Leck (1876-1958), Huzsar (1884-1960) and van Doesburg, was called "Neo-Plasticism." These artists reduced their representations into nonobjective abstractions. Curved lines were regarded as too personal. Mondrian thought he could change the condition of human life with his paintings. See Abstract Formalism and Bildarchitektur.

Still Life

An art form that can be traced to antiquity. A painting or drawing is contrived by the artist according to his interpretation of a certain theme. In rendering still life, objects are posed at close view so that the artist can study the interplay of light, form, color, and texture. Several of its formats:

- Realistic (the presentation of a subject in a detailed manner).
- Decorative (emphasis is on the overall effect rather than on separate parts).
- Symbolic (a deeper meaning is sought for the subject rather than depicting it for its own sake).
- Abstract (contrasts of colors and shapes or unusual combination of objects). See Trompe l'Oeil.

Stippling

A technique of applying color with the point of the brush in repetitive small touches of dots and points, to create a gradation of light and shade.

Stock Art

See Clip Art.

Storyboard Art

Artwork done in preparation for an animated cartoon, outlining the action of the film. It ranges anywhere from rough sketches to finished paintings in various media.

"Studio of"

A work produced under the direction of the artist. See Workshop Production.

Study

The artistic exploration of a specific subject, usually intended as a preliminary outline. See Sketch.

Style

1. A choice, either knowingly or unknowingly, by a person, school, group, or cultural age, within a certain geographical area, of a way of using components such as color, form, composition, or texture.
2. The distinctive way a thing is done in any human endeavor: a means of classification. When an artist shares certain qualities with contemporaries, it is known as a "collective" or "period" style.
3. Le style est l'homme (style is man): every artwork is shaped by a unique combination of personality traits, creative abilities, and individual, as well as national, experience.

Subjective Painting

Art that originates with the inner feelings or the spontaneity of the artist and not in accordance with reality.

Suite

A common theme depicted in several paintings: a narrative art. See Cycle Series.

Sumi Painting or Suiboku (water-ink drawing)

A Japanese term referring to a particular manner of brush painting in ink. (In China, its place of origin, it is called Shui-mo-hua.) Tonal values are created by washes from pale gray to black.

Supergraphics (1960s)

Monumental designs painted or applied to interior surfaces to give the illusion of widening space; flat outlines of geometric forms or fragments of photomurals were the usual designs. It was a kind of optical art because of the distortion created: the architectural scale seemed to change.

Super-Realism

The sculptural equivalent of this technique is seen in the work of Hanson (1925-1996), who began life-casting ordinary people, painting the sculptures in exact, realistic detail and, finally, dressing the figures in clothing the models themselves would wear in everyday life. These sculptural forms are so intense the eye can see more than it would in real life. See Urban Figures.

Support

Referring to the surface on which a painting is made such as canvas, paper, wall, or panel.

Support-Surface

A contemporary French group concerned with the material used in painting such as printed oilcloth, nylon tapestries, and plastic sheets.

Suprematism (1913-1917)

An attitude of mind rather than an art movement: Malevich (1878-1935) opined that works of art were suggestions of the subconscious mind. In his essays, he stated his new color realism should avoid any natural appearance or sensation, art should not be expressive of any emotion except pure artistic feeling and it should be created from geometric form. His nonobjective, mystical representations were used as contemplative images to attain the "zaum" state—visions of "the nonexistent revealed."

Malevich's intention was to convert Suprematism into a new system of art education. It was modernism's first completely abstract painting style. See Cubo-Futurism, Purism, and Zaum.

Surmoulage

A process in which an original wax, plaster or terra-cotta model that is no longer copyrighted can be cast into bronze and sold in editions.

The terms "recast" and "aftercast" are used to describe the surmoulaged sculpture. This expensive process makes artworks available to a larger audience, although in limited editions only, usually under 12. Sculptures are defined as reproductions after 12 recasts and must be labeled as such, according to laws designed to combat fraud.

Surrealism (going beyond reality)

A movement that gained recognition in 1924, and remained active until 1966 when the poet Andre Breton died; he was internationally recognized as the force behind Surrealism. It was part of Breton's blueprint to re-create humanism by liberating the mind of man. His ideas, however, evolved with each artist. The artists who were influenced by Freud's theories would re-create on canvas their own hidden reality in the form of a spontaneous release of imagery.

Two major types of Surrealism were distorted but recognizable, figurative forms and abstract fantasy. Techniques included the use of automatism, composed objects, found objects, and transformation.

The term "Surrealism" was coined by the writer-critic Apollinaire, who first used it in the preface of a play; his writings were also a strong influence on this movement.

Picasso (1881-1973)
Arp (1887-1966)
Savinio (1891-1952)
Ernst (1891-1976)
Miró (1893-1984)
Masson (1896-1987)
Delvaux (1897-1994)
Sage (1898-1963)
Magritte (1898-1967)
Tanguy (1900-1955)

See New World Surrealism.

Surreal Object

A progeny of Surrealism that is represented by assemblage. Other than the artist's contribution in linking the Object together, it possesses no aesthetic value or use. It might suggest the reality obtained by interpretation of the mind. Breton called it "a convulsive beauty."

Man Ray (1890-1976)
Cornell (1903-1973)
M. Oppenheimer (1913-1985)
Baron (1927-1987)

Surrender of Breda, The

Although this painting by Velásquez (1599-1660) conveys the sense of absolute truth, it is historically incorrect. It is generally recognized, nonetheless, as the greatest military picture ever painted. The scene depicted commemorates the Spanish victory over the Dutch in 1625. See War Art.

Symbol

Any kind of shape, sign, form, pattern, color, or line which is used by an artist to express abstract ideas or hidden meanings.

Symbolic art can also be vivid and elaborate in the story it tells: classic are the symbolic devices of prehistoric and ancient cultures.

Symbolism

A French movement during the last two decades of the 1800s, with manifestations in the fine arts, as well as in literature and music.

The poet Rimbaud said: "The objects given to us in our common-sense world must be converted by the artist's mystical vision into symbols of a reality beyond it."

Color, line, and rhythm linked with subject matter evocative of the esoteric, the exotic, or the mysterious resulted in paintings that resemble fantasies or dream-like meditations.

G. Moreau (1826-1898)
Redon (1840-1916)
Gauguin (1848-1903)
Hodler (1853-1918)
Toorop (1858-1928)
Klimt (1862-1918)

See Nabis and Synthetism.

Synagogue at Dura Europos (A. D. 244-245)

This synagogue, erected in Mesopotamia, was discovered in 1932 and has been reconstructed for the National Museum in Damascus. Its walls and ceiling contain paintings of Old Testament scenes, historical writings, astrological objects, animals, and flowers, all expressive of the Jewish tradition. The frescoes contained therein are the earliest representations of Old Testament scenes known to date. See Jewish Art.

Synchromism (with color) (1913-1919)

The American counterpart of Orphism formulated by M. Russell (1886-1953) and MacDonald-Wright (1890-1973). The development of color in their paintings was aided by already established principles: the law of simultaneous contrasts, the law of harmony of analogous colors, and the law of harmony of contrasts.

The artists theorized that since warm colors advance and cool colors recede, they could be used to create pictorial space and depth. Their analysis of color-form relations contributed to new abstract theories.

Synthetism (1886-1891)

This term is a secondary name for Symbolist painting; it can be described as a synthesis between real experience and inner vision. (The Symbolist poet Mallarmè told his followers "to paint not the thing itself but the effect it produces on us.")

When Gauguin was in Brittany, he and fellow artists (known as the Pont-Aven group or circle) were preoccupied with the theory and practice of art: they rejected naturalistic interpretation for a more expressive style.

The artists believed line, form, and color had their own meanings, whether or not used in recognizable imagery. Their primitive-like paintings were characterized by dark outlines, flat shapes, broad areas of color, rhythmic contours, and simple subject matter with allusion to dreams or visions. See Cloisonnism and Symbolism.

Systematic Composition

A technique that enables the viewer to define the relationship of each part to the whole, without fear of misreading the painter's scheme: everything in an artwork falls reasonably into place.

Systemic Art

Referring to art of repetitive imagery of nonrepresentational shapes, usually geometric in character.

T

Tableau d'Histoire

Classic are the sentimental illustrations of American historic scenes: national heroes and events are romanticized to the point where suffering, grief, and the wounds of war are translated into nostalgic images.

Tableau Objet

The concept developed by Picasso and Braque that a painting, as built up or constructed, has a separate life of its own in its independent attempt to re-create the external world. Essentially, the attempt to discover a trompe l'esprit. See Papier Collé.

Tableau Vivant (living picture)

A scene is presented by silent participants.

Tableaux Éclatés (exploding paintings)

Saint Phalle (1930-   ) perfected a new art form that uses electronic technology to present moving images: when a viewer approaches, a sensor causes the garishly colored, three-dimensional, cartoon-like artworks to move or come apart. See Audio-Installation Art.

Tachisme (blot, stain)

A French term, introduced in 1954, corresponding to Action Painting. Those who painted in this style placed emphasis on impulsive and unplanned effects. The artists were called "Tachistes."

Tactile Values

Referring to the illusion of three dimensionality or lifelike volume. See Texture.

Taos/Santa Fe School (1898-1927)

Although the spiritual father of this group was Sharp (1859-1953), it was not until Phillips (1868-1956) and Blumenschein (1874-1960) visited New Mexico that the region became popular for its landscape and ideal painting weather. Despite the fact that most of the first Taos painters (known as the "Original Taos Six") had undergone rigorous academic training and were professional illustrators, the grandeur of the landscape, with its brilliant light, moved the artists to paint their canvases with high-key colors and loose brushwork — in the manner of the modernists. Favored subjects were still lifes and portraiture of Pueblo Indians and Spanish Americans as well as the depiction of their everyday activities and their cultural and religious heritage. These pictures breathe the spirit of the American Southwest.

The Taos Society of Artists was formulated in 1912 to exhibit, promote, and sell the artists' paintings of New Mexico; by 1915, Taos had become a vital artists colony. By the time the Society disbanded in 1927, it had enrolled 21 artists; most of them attained a national reputation.

Over the course of the 20th century, the Taos/Santa Fe area has continued to thrive as an art center; many major American and European artists have painted there.

Tapestries

An ancient craft traced to the Egyptians.

Tapestries, made from woven materials, were usually embellished with representations of real or mythical animals, flowers, and other decorative subjects. They were also created to capture historic or momentous events, most notably during the long reign of Louis XIV in France. Their primary function, during the Middle Ages especially, was to cover walls and furniture.

The emergence of contemporary tapestry occurred in postwar France under the leadership of J. Lurcat. His ideas and influence spread throughout the US and Europe.

This craft continues to grow as a genuine form of artistic expression, as seen in the hands of weavers who create tapestries with modern or contemporary themes. See Weaving.

Technique

1. A style in which an artist uses line and color, as a poet uses words.
2. The skill of an artist in the use of a medium, as well as knowledge and mastery of the mechanics and materials used.

Tempera Painting

The application of pigment, mixed with egg yolk, egg white, and/or other substance, to panels coated with gesso. Fine detail and brilliant colors give tempera painting a jewel-like quality.

This medium was known to the Egyptians, Greeks, and Romans, but was fully developed during the Byzantine period. It was the principal medium throughout Europe until the 1500s; thereafter, it was used for an additional 200 years in Russia and other areas where the Eastern Orthodox Church was active.

Tempered

The mixture of elements in correct proportions.

Tenebrism

Referring to the effect of strong or deep shadows. It involves contrasts of light and dark for stark, dramatic effect. By the 1600s, European painters, called "Tenebrists," used violent contrasts of light and shade. See Caraviggisti.

Ten Ornaments of Nature

Leonardo da Vinci's theories of light, shade, color, body, figure, position, distance, nearness, movement, and rest in rendering artworks, particularly anatomical drawings, and in the use of techniques such as chiaroscuro or perspective.

Ten, The

A group of American Impressionists who began to exhibit together in 1898 to protest Europeanism. They constituted a kind of academy and exhibited together annually for 20 years.

The American approach to Impressionism was romantic and idealistic, and was especially suited to American landscape.

Dewing (1851-1938)	De Camp (1855-1923)
Weir (1852-1919)	Hassam (1859-1935)
Simmons (1852-1931)	Reid (1862-1929)
Twachtman (1853-1902)	Tarbell (1862-1938)
Metcalf (1853-1925)	Benson (1862-1951)

See American Impressionism.

Ten, The (1935-1940)

A group of expressionist artists of the New York School who protested the conservatism of the art establishment.

Terra-Cotta

A tile made from fired clay. It has a long history, going back to the Mycenaean period, Egypt, China, the Mayan Culture, and Greece. Renaissance sculptors used it often as an alternative to marble and stone. The finest tile is believed to come from Italy.

Terra-Cotta Army

During the 1970s in China, thousands of life-size statues of imperial warriors belonging to the Han dynasty (206 B.C.- A.D. 221) were excavated.

Texture

Tactile values such as roughness or smoothness seem almost real. The technique of realistic effect depends, in the main, on the source of light in the picture.

Texturologies (earth paintings)

These abstract, coarsely textured paintings by Dubuffet (1901-1985) re-create the surface of the earth when seen from a height. The artist's work had a strong international influence.

Thayer's Law

The artist Thayer (1849-1921) formulated a set of principles dealing with the analysis of visual phenomena. His studies led to camouflage techniques used by military forces.

Theatre Art

Classic is the work of Wilson (1941-), who creates mammoth theatre pieces of stagecraft that combine slow movement, painterly vision, and stylized articulation of narrative or song: a kind of post-modern, neo-surrealistic, visual and aural montage.

Titles of several works include *The Life and Times of Joseph Stalin, Einstein on the Beach, The Civil Wars*, and *Parsifal.*

Theorem Painting

Referring to the use of stencils in the creation of still-life compositions. The customary mediums were pastels on paper, or watercolor on paper or velvet. This American Folk art peaked in popularity from 1820 to 1840.

Thinning

Paint which is applied thinly — the opposite of impasto.

Thousand Buddha Caves

In 1990, a series of caves was discovered near Dun Huang in China. The caves, decorated with "beautifully" painted icons, had been covered with desert sand for centuries. A treasure trove of Chinese scrolls and art objects was found in the caves.

Three Dimensional

Possessing or seeming to possess the dimensions of width, height, and depth, whereby form and volume are perceived through gradations of tone, light, shadow, or proportion.

Three-Dimensional Picture

A painting executed in relief, with layers of materials. See Impasto.

Toile de Jouy (cloth of Joy)

Referring to traditional French fabric design: gardens, cozy interiors, and animal figuration.

Tôle Peinte (painted tinware)

A technique developed in the 1600s for finishing metal household goods such as plates, trays, planters, and tables. It developed into a flourishing art form in the 1700s when new discoveries were made enabling metal to hold thin coats of color. When the electroplating process was invented, tôle production ended.

Tonalism

The close arrangement or relationship of tones to create mood or the sensation of overall coloration in a painting. See American Tonalism and Macchiaioli School.

Tondo

A round painting or sculpted relief. Tondi were popular in Italy during the Renaissance.

Topographical Art

The pictorial representation of specific places or objects such as towns or country houses. See View Painting.

Tradition

The rules of art that have passed from one generation of artists to the next. Its overuse can lead to convention or pastiche. Duchamp's dictum: "Rules are fatal to the progress of art."

Trajan's Column (A. D. 113)

This sculpture, ten stories high and located in the Roman Forum, is classic of the continuous style. It is regarded as a masterpiece of Roman historical art. The stone-cutting, carried out in low relief, reveals a flow of action going from episode to episode. Similar columns were created in other cities.

In the 11th century, this art form was revived when the *Column of Bishop Bernward* was rendered to display events from Christ's life.

Tramp Art (1870s-1930s)

Wandering artisans, mostly German or Scandinavian woodworkers who had immigrated to the US, crafted elaborately embellished furniture and small objects such as framed mirrors, boxes, and clock cases. Their tools were nothing more than a pocket-knife or a handmade chisel. Payment was usually in the form of food and lodgings as the artisans traveled the countryside.

Tramp art is now regarded as Americana; art dealers have sold pieces at prices ranging from hundreds to thousands of dollars.

Transavantguardia (Trans-Avant-Gardes)

A term coined by the Italian critic Oliva in 1979 to describe those artists preoccupied with problems of the Italian past: they question, parody, and throw into disorder historic styles in general. The artists have been linked to German Neo-Expressionism.

Transformation

In Surrealism, the radical changing of objects into different shapes or forms.

Transformation-Installation

The Belgian artist Bijl (1947-) creates three-dimensional still lifes inside gallery and museum spaces in order to comment on life and consumerism in current-day society. The artist's intention is to transform reality into artifice, to fill in the space between art and life. Among these life-size, symbolic representations of Western civilization are installations titled *Drawing School, Hairdressing Salon, Gambling Casino, Fashion Boutique*, and *Fitness Center*.

Transitory Artworks

Classic is a multimillion-dollar project called "The Umbrellas, Japan-U.S.A." created by Christo (1935-) who, with the assistance of many workers, installed 3,100 19-foot-high umbrellas, each weighing approximately 480 pounds, in open areas near Tokyo and Los Angeles for a period of three weeks in 1991. It was the artist's intention to create "a symphony in two parts, where one part is fast and the other is slow." Christo was a member of the Nouveaux Réalistes.

Another short-term project, "Reichstag: Project for Berlin, 1995," by the same artist and his wife, Jeanne-Claude, involved the wrapping of the German Reichstag. Materials and labor cost almost $8.3 million.

Treasure of Sipán

The discovery in 1987 by thieves of burial chambers containing ceramic vessels, gold and silver objects, and murals, all depicting stories of the lives of the Moche people of northern Peru from A. D. 100 to 800.

Tres Grandes, Los (The Great Three)

Three famous Mexican muralists whose Arte Comprometido (see Art Engagè) served to proclaim the evils of tyranny and to emphasize the benefits of social/political revolution. The Mexican mural renaissance, which ripened after the Revolution, began to sour after 1924: a presidential decree suspended most mural production because of student riots and political upheavals. The period 1929-1934 was one of political repression; the muralists left temporarily for the US to teach and to paint.

Orozco (1883-1949), Rivera (1886-1957), and Siqueiros (1896-1974) were the principal founders of the Mexican School of Painting/Muralism. See Mural and Revolutionary Art.

Très Riches Heures du duc de Berry

The brothers Limbourg (active 1399-1439) painted a miniature picture of each month's labors and activities (calendar pictures), as well as biblical scenes, in a Book of Hours (prayer book). The pictures are highly accurate in detail and offer the entire spectrum of religious beliefs, as well as scenes of both nature and society. The pages contained in this bookwork are regarded as the most beautiful incunabulum of Northern European art of this period; it has been referred to as the "fountainhead of Western landscape painting."

Tressage (braiding)

A term adopted by Rouan (1943-   ) to describe a unique painting technique invented by him. It consists of interweaving vertical/horizontal strips from two canvases painted in various colors on which he paints a new pattern.

Triptych

1. An artwork in three parts.
2. A panel painting consisting of three sections: a central piece and two wings which are hinged to fold over the central panel. During centuries past, the triptych usually served as an altarpiece.

Trojan Gold Treasure (1250 B.C.)

A treasure consisting of 12,000 objects, including coins, jewelry, and vessels, crafted from gold, and currently believed to be worth a billion dollars. The treasure was uncovered in 1873 by an archeologist in Turkey and brought to Germany; it disappeared during WWII and is now located in Russia. The German and Turkish governments have made demands for the return of this treasure.

Trompe l'Oeil (deceives the eye)

A highly traditional and decorative style of painting and interior decoration. Everyday objects, such as mugs, tobacco, books, and newspapers, are posed and painted with painstaking and meticulous technique. Flat surfaces appear three dimensional: the illusion of reality is obtained by eliminating any sign of the surface quality of the canvas —absolute smoothness of surface is required. Another technique is to create very shallow space.

Goodwin (1840-1910)	Pope (1849-1924)
Harnett (1848-1892)	Peto (1854-1907)

A more recent artist of this genre is Haas (1936-), who in 1974 started to paint trompe l'oeil murals on buildings throughout the US. His murals are now regarded as major public art.

20th Century Art

It is occasionally referred to as "Since Cézanne," who was the forerunner of Cubism and Abstract art. He is now regarded as the key to Modern art.

Artists have always sought to change, to renew, or to be influenced by other artists, but it is only in this century that art has changed so rapidly. (The pace of development in other aspects of society, however, has been just as rapid.)

The first major change was the reversal of traditional ideas that art should portray beauty and the realities of the world. Another important factor in turning away from representational painting was the advancement of photography. The artist felt he had to find a newer, more original role. With the invention of new materials, the artist was able to explore new art forms.

Two-Dimensional Painting

Before the development of perspective, pictures appeared lifeless and flat. In Modern art, instead of using perspective, subjects are spaced and they diminish in size according to distance. The background seems to move forward.

291 Group (1905-1917)

A group of artists who exhibited at the photo studio operated by Stieglitz (1864-1946) in Manhattan. Stieglitz looked forward to new developments. He held about 80 exhibitions in his studio to promote the work of American artists Demuth, Dove, Marin, and O'Keeffe, among others. He also introduced to America the work of Braque, Cézanne, Matisse, Picasso, and others. When his studio closed in 1917, he continued exhibitions at two other galleries — Intimate Gallery (1925-1929) and An American Place (1929-1946); both galleries promoted American artists only.

U

Ukiyo-e (scenes from the passing world)

A Japanese term referring to the depiction of people engaged in everyday activities. It was a trend that began in the 1600s; woodcut prints were the usual means of production. Harunobu (1725-1770) was probably one of the most prolific artists of this genre. It was he who developed Nishiki-e, a technique of polychrome printmaking from wood blocks. Formerly, only a few colors were used.

After 1800, artists began to shift to the ephemeral aspects of landscape, as seen in the works of Hokusai (1760-1849) and Hiroshige (1797-1858).

Japanese prints became popular in the Western world and were influential on numerous artists of the School of Paris, most notably Cassatt, Degas, Gauguin, Monet, Toulouse-Lautrec, and van Gogh: Japanese techniques were incorporated into Western art traditions. See Mitate.

Umbrian School

Piero della Francesca (1416-1492)
Bonfiglio (1420-1496)
Da Forli (1438-1494)
Antoniazzo (1440-1526)
Perugino (1446-1523)
Pintoricchio (1454-1513)
Raphael (1483-1520)
Barocci (1535-1612)

Underground, the

The underground artist feels himself alienated and wants to set up a new society, especially as seen in recent decades in the former Soviet Union and other non-democratic countries. In the Soviet Union, art unacceptable to the official art establishment was called "Nonconformist art."

Unexpressionism

An art of the non-being and the insignificant. Everyday life in its repetition and lack of originality is studied and stripped. Artificial images are constructed and juxtaposed: the emptiness of context seems to be the motif.

Unit One (1933-1935)

A British group whose only commonality was they stood for the expression of a contemporary spirit in painting, sculpture, and architecture. It had a strong impact on British art.

Unity

The quality of oneness or harmony which enables the viewer to perceive the motif. Vital interaction is basic to the perception of unity.

Urban Figures

Classic is the work of Segal (1924-) who creates ghostly plaster figures incorporated into eerily lifelike scenes that seem to suggest some kind of silent communication.

In the 19th century, the sculptor Rogers (1829-1904) created over 80 plaster groups of people in action: everyday events, scenes from the Civil War, literature, and sports. They were very popular and sometimes as many as 12,000 copies of a group were reproduced from molds.

Utrecht School

A group of Dutch painters who were in Rome for a decade (1610-1620), and who worked together in Utrecht. Under the influence of Caravaggio and Manfredi, they used religious and genre themes.

V

Value

The relation of one part of a picture to another part with regard to lightness and darkness. See Chiaroscuro.

Vanishing Point

A point at which something disappears, an important element of linear perspective when parallel lines meet in order to obtain the illusion of depth and distance.

Vanitas

The use of objects in a painting as a reminder of the vanity of life or the passing of earthly life with its attendant pleasures and achievements. It may include a skull, instruments of destruction, perishable items, or the objects and materials of wealth to reflect on the futility of riches: a kind of moral message. This genre was popular in Western Europe during the 1500s/1600s. Classic is the work of de Heem (1606-1684) of the Dutch School.

The Cubist artist Braque (1882-1963) painted a series of paintings titled *Vanitas*; they contain symbols of the spiritual and material worlds. See Memento Mori.

Variant

See Copy.

Varnish

A transparent liquid film applied to a painting to protect it and to give it a certain gloss.

Vassar College

In 1865, this school became the first institution to open with a gallery and collection.

Veduta

The representation of a known landscape or town. Classic are 137 illustrated sights of Rome, titled *Vedute di Roma*, rendered by Piranesi (1720-1778). See View Painting.

Vehicle

The liquid in which pigments are dispersed to make a paint. See Medium.

Veils

Louis (1912-1962) poured thinned pigment onto canvas, then placed it on a vertical scaffolding and allowed it to hang free. The paint flowed down over the surface in rhythmic curves, guided by folds the artist made in the canvas. Using wash after wash of extremely thinned acrylic, these misty, diaphanous, and soft effects resulted in pure color compositions. See Stain Painting.

Venetian School

Jacobello (1394-1439)
J. Bellini (1400-1471)
Ant. Vivarini (1415-1480)
Gentile Bellini (1429-1507)
Messina (1430-1479)
B. Vivarani (1430-1491)
Crivelli (1430-1495)
Giovanni Bellini (1430-1516)
Alv. Vivarini (1446-1505)
DeRoberti (1456-1496)
Carpaccio (1465-1526)
Giorgione (1478-1510)
Lotto (1480-1556)
Titian (1490-1576)
Tintoretto (1518-1594)
Veronese (1528-1588)
Balestra (1666-1740)
Piazzetta (1683-1745)
Tiepolo (1696-1770)
Canaletto (1697-1768)
Longhi (1702-1785)
Guardi (1712-1793)

Venice Biennale

The world's oldest international art exhibition, founded by the city of Venice in 1895, which continues to this day. Its foundation is the presentation of artworks from many countries and the awarding of prizes. In 1990, it celebrated its 44th exhibition with 46 countries represented. The 45th biennial had 53 countries represented by 735 artists. (Over 100 years, more than 50,000 artists have been shown.)

The great number of artists, collectors, and dealers attending has made it the most popular and most august of all international exhibitions.

Verifax Collage

A primitive copy process used by Berman (1926-1976) between 1964 and 1976 for the creation of small, negative and positive, surreal-like and mythical prints, arranged in grids of four to 64 units, sometimes accompanied by scribbled notes or Hebrew letters. Berman was a member of a movement called California Assemblage.

Verism

1. The concept that everyday events have their own worth, as opposed to romantic themes.
2. A disturbing Realism associated with the New Objectivity movement.

Video Arbor by Paik (1932-)

Perhaps the first permanent video installation. It consists of 84 TV monitors, mounted on 24 columns, with pictures of fish and flowers and scenes of Philadelphia. Its locale is an apartment complex. (Paik was the first artist in the early 1960s to test the tube as a new medium, and he is often referred to as the father of Video art.)

Video Art

Basically, a new expressive art ritual using high tech for the creation of tapes of moving images of abstract or representational compositions, with or without sound, often combined with assemblage, constructions, performances, or sculptural tableaux. Its primary value lies in its efficiency as a channel of communication and as a commentary on the times.

Lucier (1944-) said: "Video installations do everything I am interested in as an artist. They're three dimensional and include elements of theatre, sculpture, and Performance art." See Audio Installation Art.

Videopavilion

The union of architecture and popular art: architectural space, video, and music are brought together by deconstructivist architects in inventive, fantastically designed pavilions or structures.

View Painting / Veduta

A highly developed art in 18th-century Italy, especially Venice, when well-known tourist meccas and famous ruins were realistically depicted.

Panini (1691-1765)	Guardi (1712-1793)
Canaletto (1697-1768)	Piranesi (1720-1778)
	Bellotto (1720-1780)

See Capriccios.

Virtual Gallery

Viewers can see an artist's work on a simulated wall (presented on a CD-ROM), zoom in for a closer look, get a biography of the artist, and find out how to buy the work. Classic is the work of Csuri (1923-), who is recognized as the master of a new medium. His computer images are full of mystery, myth, symbol, and ritual, all ancient elements of art. See Computer Art.

Virtual Reality

A term describing a dream-like computer world that reacts to a viewer's real-world actions. By moving in front of a video camera linked to a computer, one's silhouette is projected onto one of dozens of colorful, fantastical, and imaginative scenarios. It enables human consciousness to reach beyond ordinary reality into expanded experience and knowledge; in practical terms, realistic environments are generated by computers. See Cyberspace.

Aside from entertainment purposes, virtual reality is used as a tool for training programs to simulate activities, to improve the lives of disabled persons, and to overcome phobias such as fear of heights.

Visionary Architecture

Rather than bricks and mortar, the materials used are ink and paper. Traditionally, architects have turned to visionary designs to project utopian futures, to revisit the past, or to explore the imagination. See Capriccios.

Visionary Art Museum

This museum, located in Baltimore, and designated as the official national visionary art museum by congressional resolution in 1992, is the first American facility devoted exclusively to the work of self-taught artists. See Outsider Art.

Visionary Imagists

A contemporary group of painters and sculptors in Louisiana, whose meticulous, figurative artworks are expressive of subjects ranging from the ecological crisis to God. Their so-called visions also contain fantastical and humorous motifs.

Visual Artists Rights Act of 1990

The first federal moral rights law enacted to protect the work of artists and to enforce artists' rights.

Visual Realism

The capture of the impact of life in its immediacy: the quality of truth at maximum intensity is recognized at first glance.

Vita Brevis, Ars Longa.

Life is short, art is long.

Vita Sine Ars Mors Est.

Life without art is death.

Vitruvian Figure

The allegation during Renaissance years that man's proportions are perfect because with his arms and legs extended he would fit perfectly into geometric forms such as the circle or the square.

In more recent times, Giovanopoulos (1939-   ) has rendered a triptych, titled *Universal Man* I, II, and III, in which the Vitruvian Man is depicted in a series of 75 thematic grid paintings.

Vollard Suite

A series of 46 etchings rendered by Picasso (1881-1973) in which he depicts himself, most often as a minotaur (half man, half bull). Greek potters often illustrated the minotaur on their pots.

Vorticism (1913-1920)

An English movement formed by Lewis (1884-1957) as an outgrowth of Cubism and Futurism. Paintings and drawings by the artists reveal they were engaged in creating abstract, geometric compositions, with accent on contrasts and tensions, to depict the energies of life. Lewis defined Vorticism in general terms as "Activity, Significance, and Essential Movement." His theory was that dynamic energy moved quickly through successive images into a depth — a vortex. See Orphism.

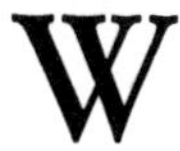

Wall Painting

A painting executed in any medium, usually fresco, on a prepared wall. Many of the earliest paintings were made on cave walls. In ancient civilizations, large murals covering temples, tombs, and palaces were an integral part of architectural decoration. Mural painting was popular in Italy; classic are the cycle frescoes found in churches and public buildings. See Cycle Series, Fresco, and Mural.

Wanderers, The (1870s-1920s)

A Russian movement, formed in order to bring Realism to the people, especially depicting the sufferings of the poor and the oppressed.

War Art

- Goya (1746-1828) rendered a series of etchings, titled *Disasters of War*, in which he violently depicts the atrocities committed in wartime.
- Walker (1819-1889) is known for his battle scenes of both the Mexican and Civil Wars.
- Rosenthal (1833-1918) was an official illustrator for the US Military Commission during the Civil War.
- Homer (1836-1910) depicted genre scenes from the Civil War.
- X. R. Smith (1839-1929) painted battle scenes of the Civil War.
- Gaul (1855-1919) painted many scenes of the American West, but his Civil War pictures were especially admired for their accuracy.
- Sargent (1856-1925) painted in the battle area during WWI. Among his paintings are *The Arrival of American Troops at the Front, France* and *Gassed.*
- Trego (1859-1909) specialized in historically accurate battle scenes, ranging from the American Revolution to the Franco-Prussian War, with particular emphasis on the Civil War.
- Remington (1861-1909) expected to "discover the glories of war" when he illustrated scenes from the Spanish-American War.
- Picasso (1881-1973) expressed his condemnation of the Spanish Civil War with *Guernica* and of the Korean War with *Massacre in Korea.*
- Stoops (1887-1948) made drawings of tired and grimy soldiers at the front during WWI while he served as a soldier.
- Pippin (1888-1946) painted the grim details of his war experiences in WWI. His most famous military painting is *The Ending of the War: Starting Home.*
- P. Nash (1889-1946) executed drawings of "the landscape of war" at the front during WWI.
- Nevinson (1889-1946) recorded his wartime experiences on canvas.
- Dix (1891-1969) rendered 50 etchings, titled *The War*, which reflect a bitter, anti-war statement in contrast to his former belief that war had some value.
- Fautrier (1898-1964) rendered *Otages*, a series of paintings inspired by the horrors of war.

- Piper (1903-1992) painted pictures of bomb-devastated buildings during WWII.
- Bohrod (1907-1992) sketched and painted battle scenes in the Pacific and in Europe during WWII when he worked in the Army War Art Unit.
- Music (1909-) rendered a series of etchings and paintings titled *We Are Not the Last*; they relate to his imprisonment in Dachau during 1944-1945.
- Guttuso (1912-1987) published a book of anti-Nazi drawings, titled *Gott Mit Uns*, in 1944.
- Motherwell (1915-1991) created well over 100 paintings, small drawings, and sketches, titled *Elegy to the Spanish Republic*, commemorating the Spanish Civil War.
- Golub (1922-) paints pictures of rioters, mercenaries, torturers, and death-squad goons.
- Lüpertz (1941-) uses the imagery of war and its paraphernalia as provocative symbols of Germany's past.
- Kiefer (1945-) whose main topic is 12 years of organized Nazi terror.

Wash Drawing or Pen-and-Ink Drawing

A drawing executed with many dilutions of ink or monochromatic watercolor. It is often used in combination with other drawing media such as charcoal, chalk, or pencil, and is particularly effective in rendering light and shadow.

Washington Crossing the Delaware

A popular allegorical painting by Leutze (1816-1868) and probably the best-known American-history painting. Many 19th-century paintings created sentimentalized and inaccurate reconstructions of American history. See Tableau d'Histoire.

Watercolor

In its broadest sense, watercolor is any paint that is water based; essential ingredients are pigments, binding agent, and water. Its most distinct quality is transparency, making it possible to achieve delicate, luminous effects. It is a medium particularly suited to painting in plein air, requiring only a minimum of equipment and little preparation of materials.

Watercolor was the medium of classical Chinese painting and was used as early as the 3rd century B. C. for painting on silk. Dürer of the German School began the history of watercolor in the Western world. It was used, especially during centuries past, for illuminated manuscripts, for making accurate plant and animal studies, for miniature paintings, for illustration of written reports by explorers, and by tourists who wanted to record their travels.

Wax Paint

The pigment is mixed with beeswax to create a substance used for impasto.

Wax Portraits

Portrait-making on wood panels, following a naturalistic technique. It was a common practice in Egyptian and Greek art.

Weaving

The creation of a fabric is seen as a composition of colors and textures. Many textile workers believe that the greatest weavers the world has ever seen came from the Peruvian cultures that thrived before the Spanish conquest in the 1530s.

Currently, weavings created during decades or centuries past throughout the world are selling for thousands of dollars.

Weir Farm National Historic Site

The first historic site dedicated to an American artist. The farm, located in Branchville, Connecticut, was the homestead of the Impressionist Weir (1852-1919), who purchased it for $10 and one of his paintings. It is the only intact home, studio, and landscape of American Impressionism.

Western and Indian Painting

Artists played a significant role in settling the frontier, using paint to record the adventures of government surveyors, trappers, prospectors, farmers, the military, pioneers, cowboys, explorers, Indians, and the railroad, thereby capturing the imagination of the nation.

Many artists living and working in the West today root their work deeply in the tradition of the Western genre — realistic depictions of the land and people, both contemporary and historic. See History Painting, Indian Gallery, and *Sketches*.

Whirligig

A wind toy similar to a weather vane: a carved figure with moving parts powered by the wind, used mostly for decorative purposes or amusement. See Folk Art.

White Mountain Painters (1838-1911)

When access to the mountains of New Hampshire became easier in the 1800s, artists began using the mountains as subject matter for their artworks. Although many of the artists of the Hudson River School painted there, White Mountain artists are regarded as a separate group. They presented the landscape to reflect their love of nature and pride in their country.

Wildlife and Natural History

The creation of representational paintings that capture the spirit and the natural beauty of animals, fish, birds, and the great outdoors. Classic is the work of Wilson (1766-1813) and Audubon (1785-1851). This style continues to flourish in the contemporary age. See Birds of America.

Women Artists in Revolution (W.A.R.)

A so-called radical group formed in 1969 to pressure museums and commercial galleries to exhibit the work of women artists. See Guerrilla Girls.

Wood Carving

The carving of wood to create relief sculptures or objects in the round. Also, an object of wood so fashioned. The practice of wood carving dates back some 5,000 years.

Woodcut or Woodblock Print

Referring to pictorial designs printed from hand-cut blocks of wood, known as relief printing, originating in China, and used principally to produce inexpensive editions of pictures. Until Dürer of the German School refined the process, woodcuts were comparatively crude. With the development of polychrome printmaking, the Japanese brought it to a higher level. German Expressionists and other modernists, namely, Gauguin and Picasso, used the technique extensively as a form of artistic expression. See Ukiyo-e.

Word-Art

The experimental composition of words which may appear to have no meaning; strictly speaking, their meanings are only secondary to the word-images. See Art & Language and Conceptual Art.

Word-Pictures

Waldo (1958-) uses slogans, headlines, songs, old movies, memory, and dreams as sources for wry, irreverent phrases that are stenciled with spray paint on canvases, furniture, painted ceramics, and other everyday objects.

Work of Art

Referring to an artwork of high artistic quality: the expression of complex ideas inspired by the artist's perception and experience, and the intensity and significance of effect on the viewer. It possesses its own life and meaning.

According to art historian F. Hartt, four factors are involved in the formation of any artwork: purpose, style, iconography, and historical position.

Workshop Production

An artwork produced under the supervision of an artist. See Altarpiece and Atelier.

Works on Paper

A generic term that includes fine prints, drawings, watercolors, photographs, illustrated books, and architectural renderings: anything of an artistic nature that is produced on paper.

World Monuments Fund/Watch

This organization was founded in 1965 by private citizens concerned about the accelerating destruction of important art treasures, historic buildings, and architectural structures throughout the world. To date, it has completed more than 65 major projects in 20 countries.

Recently this organization has intensified its efforts through the creation of an "endangered-species list" of sites most in need of protection and repair.

World of Art (1890s)

A Russian movement embracing art, music, and poetry. It promoted modern Western styles, especially Impressionism, in contrast to the aims of The Wanderers.

Worm's-Eye View

A scene depicted as though observed from below, especially suited for portraying things that are seen looking up. Classic is *St. James Led to Martyrdom* by Mantegna (1431-1506), which is seen in sharp receding perspective.

WPA (Works Progress Administration, later called Work Projects Administration)

Post offices, schools, community centers, state capitols, and publications were filled with federally sponsored images of the Great Depression era: unemployed or heroic workers, family life, abandoned farms, closed factories, and public works projects. See Federal Art Project, Public Buildings Administration, and Public Works of Art Project.

Z

Zaum

A Cubo-Futurist language of the future that would convey knowledge "beyond the mind." Malevich (1878-1935) hoped his paintings would serve as visual expressions of zaum perceptions. See Suprematism.

Zen 49 (1950s)

A German movement belonging to the Art Informel School. Their Oriental philosophy, in reaction to Nazi anti-culture of previous years, extolled a new art of abstraction and spontaneity. The artists used automatic, calligraphic techniques as a means of attaining spiritual sublimation. See Tachisme.

Zero Group (1957-1966)

A group of German artists who were interested in kineticism and luminism. They wanted to explore the effects of color and light. The term "zero" refers to turning back of the clock in history to the year zero (a simpler age); their philosophy called for "a new idealism" and a desire to work with nature.

"Zip" Painting

The Abstract Expressionist Newman (1905-1970) painted flat fields of color divided by a band to invite a central viewing position and contemplation of the surrounding field. Various meanings have been attributed to the "zip": the Divine Light, the representation of order, and so on. See Color Field Painting.

Color Vocabulary

Achromatic

Possessing no hue: a neutral; black, gray or white.

Advancing Colors

Any warm, strong or "hot" color that appears to come forward.

Analogous colors

See Related Colors.

Atmospheric Color

Although an object may be locally colored, it is broken into hues, tints, and reflections of other colors because of light and proximity. In essence, an object is perceived to be the color it seems to be at any given moment.

Calm Color

Equality between warm and cool colors; equality between dark and light tones.

Cast

1. Modification of color by adding a trace of hue.
2. A minute difference in color only visible on close examination.

Color

Color is simply defined as the sensation produced in the eye by light rays (reflected light). The main dimensions of color are hue, intensity, tone, and temperature.

Colorist

An artist who is known for his/her use of colors.

Color Wheel

A continuous range or sequence of colors resulting from the study of light by Isaac Newton. The 12 colors on the wheel consist of primary, secondary, and tertiary values; all other colors are regarded as variations of these colors and hues. Primary colors are red, blue and yellow; secondary colors are emerald green, orange, and violet; tertiary colors are red/orange, yellow/orange, yellow/green, blue/green, blue violet, and red/violet. Colors on one side of the wheel are cool and on the other side warm.

Complementary Colors

Each primary color has a complementary color which is produced by mixing the other two primary colors. The complementary color of red is green, a mixture of blue and yellow. The complementary color of blue is orange, a mixture of yellow and red. The complementary color of yellow is violet, a mixture of red and blue.

Red and green are opposite to each other on the color wheel, as are blue and orange, yellow and violet.

One complementary color completes and intensifies the other complementary color. If two complementary colors are used in equal proportions, the warm color will appear to dominate.

Cool Color

Derived from ice: blue, green, and violet.

Day-Glo Colors

A trade name for fluorescent colors: intense, daylight colors that have a glowing effect.

Decorative Colors

They tend to be chosen for their restful and pleasing traits, as well as for their "in" style.

Diffraction Colors

The colors that are produced when light passes through a surface.

Equal Tones

Various colors with the same brightness, darkness, or other equal measurement.

Factors of Color

—Hue/tint
—Shade/intensity
—Effect of color in relation to other colors, atmosphere, distance, and light

Half-tone

A shade of gray or a color whose value is halfway between the darkest and lightest tone of that color.

Harmonizing Colors

1. Colors close to each other in warmth or coolness.
2. The same hue in different tints or shades.

Hue

1. The distinctive characteristic of a given color.
2. A general word for the shade or tint of any color.
3. The color of anything identified by a common theme: a green is seen as bluish or yellowish; a brown is cool (greenish) or warm (reddish). It may also be designated by reference to a subject: sky blue, cherry red.

Kaleidoscope

An enlivened pattern of various colors.

Key

The characteristic color and tone of a painting. Light, bright colors are high-key colors; dark tones are low key.

Local Color

1. The color of an object without consideration of the effect of light or atmosphere.
2. The color usually attributed to a certain object: red apple, blue sky.

Modulating Color

The adjustment of one area of color to an adjacent color.

Monochromatic

A color that can be seen in its various hues, tints or shades. See Related Colors.

Muted Color

Toned down or softened with a bit of gray or brown pigment.

Neutral Colors

1. Colors which range from white to black, including off-white and brown.
2. Nonassertive colors.
3. Neither warm nor cool.

Nonfigurative Color

The disregard of the known world in favor of the independence of color as an energetic force affecting the senses, a vital teaching in Modern art.

Nuance

The fine distinction in shades and tints of colors.

Opaque

Not accessible to light — the opposite of transparent.

Optical Mixture

Refer to main section.

Pastels

Soft colors produced by adding white.

Pigment

A substance used for coloring derived from various sources such as the earth, stones, minerals, animals, and vegetables. In modern times, many pigments are artificially produced.

Poster or Show Card Colors
Inexpensive opaque colors made with a water soluble binder.

Primary Colors
The pure colors of red, blue, and yellow which are the source for all other colors.

Prismatic Color
Highly colored; brilliant.

Psychedelic Colors
Fluorescent; bright and glowing colors.

Pure Color
A color that is not mixed with other colors; spectrum color.

Realistic Color
The exact, detailed color used to depict scenes from life, as opposed to painting of atmospheric color.

Related Colors
Various hues, tints, or shades of the same color (monochromatic) or colors adjacent to each other on the color wheel (analogous).

Scrambled Colors
Oil colors that are lightly mixed on the palette with a brush, resulting in a lively effect rather than that which results from carefully blended colors.

Secondary Colors
The compounds of two primary colors producing a secondary color. The colors green, orange, and violet are obtained by mixing primary colors: red and yellow equal secondary orange; red and blue equal secondary violet; yellow and blue equal secondary green. See Color Wheel and Spectrum.

Shade
1. The absence of illumination in a picture indicated by a color or a tone.
2. The varying tones of any color of the spectrum produced by mixing the color with gray, black or white or with its complement.
3. A full degree of difference between colors.

Shading
The perception of changes in tones of light and dark to obtain a three-dimensional quality. Thousands of minute gradations are seen between pure white and pure black.

Simultaneous Contrast

The way two colors act upon each other.

Spectrum

A beam of light through a glass prism results in bands of color resembling the colors of the rainbow: red, orange, yellow, blue/green, blue/violet, and violet.

Split Complement

A color and two hues on either side of its complement. Yellow is the complement of violet. The two hues analogous to violet are red/violet and blue/violet. Therefore, the split complement would be yellow, blue/violet, and red/violet.

Symbolic Colors

Certain colors have their own connotations such as black for lack of innocence or mourning, white for joy or purity, red for energy and fervor, and so on. Colors have different meanings in other countries.

Symbolist Colors

Sharply in opposition to reality. The painter expresses his feelings about the theme rather than what he sees.

Tertiary Colors

Colors that are made up of equal parts of primary and secondary colors. They are obtained by mixing a primary color and its adjacent secondary color. See Color Wheel.

Tint

A color that has been mixed with white to lighten it.

Tonal Value

The gradation or arrangement of one color from light to dark so that a relationship exists.

Tone

The quality of a color measured by value and saturation.

Tormented Color

In oil painting, a color that has been excessively worked — the opposite of freshness or brilliance.

Transparent

Fine or sheer enough to be seen through — the opposite of opaque.

Triadic Harmony

Three colors equally distant from each other on the color wheel — red, blue, and yellow or any other combination.

Value

The value of a pigment is measured by lightness or brightness. To change a value, either black or white is mixed with the color to render its value dark or light. A darkish hue would be low in value; a light hue would be high in value.

Warm Color

Derived from fire and sunshine: red, orange, and yellow.

Bibliography

World of Art Series (Thames and Hudson, Ltd.)

Boardman, J.	*Greek Art*
Dube, W. D.	*The Expressionists*
Levey, M.	*From Giotto to Cézanne: A Concise History of Painting*
Lucie-Smith, E.	*Movements in Art Since 1945*
Moszynska, A.	*Abstract Art*
Pool, P.	*Impressionism*
Stanley-Baker, J.	*Japanese Art*
Wheeler, M.	*Roman Art and Architecture*

* * * * *

Baker & Baker	*Family Treasury of Art* (Galahad Books, 1981)
Batterberry, M.	*Twentieth Century Art* (McGraw-Hill Company, 1970)
Bearden & Henderson	*Six Black Masters of American Art* (Doubleday, 1972)
Boas, N.	*Society of Six* (Bedford Arts, 1988)
Canaday, J.	*Mainstreams of Modern Art* (Simon & Schuster, 1959)
Cole & Gealt	*Art of the Western World* (Summit Books, 1989)
Craven, T.	*Men of Art* (Simon & Schuster, 1931)
Davidson, M. B.	*A History of Art* (Random House, 1984)
Field, D. M.	*Great Masterpieces of World Art* (The Hamlyn Publishing Group, 1979)
Gaunt, W.	*A Concise History of English Painting* (Frederick A. Praeger, 1964)
Gombrich, E. H.	*The Story of Art* (Phaidon Press, 1978)
Goodrich, L.	*Three Centuries of American Art* (Frederick A. Praeger, 1966)
Haggar, R. H.	*A Dictionary of Art Terms* (New Orchard Editions, Inc., 1984)
Heller, N. G.	*Women Artists: An Illustrated History* (Abbeville Press, 1991)
Honnef, K.	*Contemporary Art* (Taschen, 1988)
Hunter & Jacobus	*Modern Art* (Harry N. Abrams, Inc., 1992)
Janson, H. W.	*A Basic History of Art* (Prentice-Hall, Inc., 1980)
Lucie-Smith, E.	*Art in the Eighties* (Phaidon Universe, 1990)
Lynton, N.	*The Story of Modern Art* (Cornell University Press, 1980)
McLanathan, R.	*The American Tradition in the Arts* (Harcourt, Brace & World, Inc., 1968)
Myron & Sundell	*Art in America: From Colonial Days Through the 19th Century* (The Macmillan Company, 1969)
Picon, G.	*Modern Painting from 1800 to the Present* (Newsweek Books, 1974)
Piper, D.	*Looking at Art* (Random House, 1984)
Rabb, T. K.	*Renaissance Lives: Portrait of an Age* (Pantheon Books, 1993)
Read, H.	*A Concise History of Modern Painting* (Praeger Publishers, 1972)

Sargent, W. *The Enjoyment and Use of Color* (Dover Publications, 1964)

Schaffner, C. *Discovering American Folk Art* (Harry N. Abrams, 1991)

Selz, P. *Art in Our Times: A Pictorial History of 1890-1980* (Harry N. Abrams, Inc., 1981)

Shone, R. *The Post-Impressionists* (Gallery Books, 1979)

Vincent, J. *History of Art* (Barnes & Noble, 1955)

Watson, D. *The Techniques of Painting* (Galahad Books, 1970)

Wentinck, C. *Masterpieces of Art: 450 Treasures of Europe* (Park Lane)

* * * * *

African-American Artists (1880-1987) Smithsonian Institution (1989)

American Art Analog I, II, and III Compiled by M. Zellman (The Chelsea House Publishers, 1986)

Concepts of Modern Art Edited by N. Stangos (Harper & Row, 1981)

Encyclopedia of American Art E. P. Dutton (1981)

Figure in 20th Century American Art, The Selections from the Metropolitan Museum of Art (1984)

Gardner's Art Through the Ages Harcourt Brace Jovanovich (1975)

Great Paintings Edited by E. Mullins (St. Martin's Press, 1981)

Illustrated Encyclopedia of Western Art, The Exeter Books (1979)

Impressionism Chartwell Books (1973)

Italian Art in the 20th Century: Painting and Sculpture 1900-1985 Edited by E. Braun (Prestel-Verlag and Royal Academy of Arts, 1989)

Major European Art Movements 1900-1945 Edited by Kaplan & Manso (E. P. Dutton, 1977)

Master Paintings from the Phillips Collection Shorewood Fine Art Books (1981)

McGraw-Hill Dictionary of Art Edited by S. Myers (1969)

New International Illustrated Encyclopedia of Art, The Greystone Press (1967-1971)

New Painting, The: Impressionism 1874-1886 The Fine Arts Museum of San Francisco (1986)

Oxford Companion to Twentieth-Century Art, The Edited by H. Osborne (Oxford University Press, 1981)

Popular History of the Arts, A Cavendish House (1968)

Seven Centuries of Art Time-Life Books (1972)

Spiritual in Art, The: Abstract Painting (1890-1985) Los Angeles County Museum of Art and Abbeville Press (1987)

Treasury of Art Masterpieces, A Edited by T. Craven (Simon & Schuster, 1966)

World Art Treasures Edited by G. Hindley (Octopus Books, 1979)

* * * * *

American Artist

American Art Review

Art & Antiques

ARTnews

Connoisseur

High Performance

National Geographic

School Arts

Smithsonian

Sun Storm Fine Art

The New York Times